How Technical
Analysis Works

Bruce M. Kamich

New York Institute of Finance
An Imprint of Prentice Hall Press
A member of Penguin Putnam Inc.

NYIF and NEW YORK INSTITUTE OF FINANCE are trademarks of Executive Tax Reports, Inc. used under license by Prentice Hall Direct, Inc.

This publication is designed to provide accurate and authoritative information in regard to the subject matter covered. It is sold with the understanding that the publisher is not engaged in rendering legal, accounting, or other professional service. If legal advice or other expert assistance is required, the services of a competent professional person should be sought.
—From the Declaration of Principles jointly adopted by a Committee of the American Bar Association and a Committee of Publishers and Associations.

Printed in the United States of America

10 9

ISBN 0-7352-0270-2

This book is dedicated to Barnet Kamich,
my father of blessed memory,
who would have been so proud to see his son published.
My father was a lover of books
and knew firsthand how an education
could change your life.

Acknowledgments

I want to thank everyone who had a hand directly and indirectly in the publication of this book.

I was first exposed to technical analysis in an investment course in 1972 at the University of Connecticut, but my real love for the subject was not kindled until I took a course with Ralph Acampora. Ralph is an amazing teacher who can get you excited about charts and the market—anyone who ever takes his course has to leave it with an appreciation and love for the craft. Alan Shaw is another teacher who needs thanking because he gets you to really look at indicators and teaches you to ask questions of the market and yourself.

All the students I have taught at Rutgers University and Baruch College and elsewhere need some acknowledgment— they gave me immediate feedback if I tried to explain something and it was not clear. So if the ideas presented in this book are easy to understand, we can thank the hundreds of undergraduates and graduate students who stayed awake three evenings a week to get their first introduction to technical analysis. As part of the course requirement, each student has to review five Web sites during the semester. Some of the best sites they found are listed below. One student stands out—my youngest son, Mark, is a recent graduate with a degree in finance. He read many of the early drafts and proofread the galley proof.

Thanks goes to the companies and people who supplied the charts and illustrations—www.prophetfinance.com, www.pfr. com, www.recognia.com, Kenneth G. Tower of CyberTrader, A Charles Schwab Company, Paul F. Desmond of Lowry's Reports, Inc., and Edward Dobson of Traders Press, Inc. A thank you also goes to Shelley Lebeck, the administrative officer of the Market Technicians Association, who allowed me to keep several books out from the MTA Library for longer than normal.

Special thanks goes to Steve Nison who wrote two books on candlesticks and found time in his busy schedule to write the Foreword and to give me periodic pep talks to keep me on track to finish this book. Steve also put in a few good words for me with the staff at Prentice Hall who took a gamble on a first-time author for this subject. This brings us to the staff at Prentice Hall. It's the job of Ellen Coleman and Sybil Grace to work with authors every day, and they do it in a professional and understanding manner.

Anyone who writes a book and neglects his spouse for two years must have a strong marriage and a very understanding partner. If this book could have a double byline my wife, Susan, would get top billing. Susan helped with the computer files and the illustrations; she read nearly every chapter and was my sounding board for ideas.

Susan optimistically labeled the file on the computer "Bruce's First Book." We'll see.

Contents

5 THE KEY BUILDING BLOCKS OF SUPPORT AND RESISTANCE   65

6 PATTERNS TO PROFIT BY   83

7 REVERSALS CAN KEEP YOU ON YOUR TOES   109

8 CONSOLIDATIONS ARE GREAT ENTRY POINTS   125

9 GAPS: WHAT'S NOT THERE IS WHAT'S IMPORTANT   149

18 OVERCOMING THE PITFALLS: REAL-WORLD TECHNICAL ANALYSIS 257

19 PUTTING IT ALL TOGETHER: CASE STUDIES 265

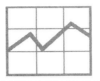

Foreword

"To hear it told is not equal to experience"
—Japanese proverb

I have known Bruce Kamich for more than twenty-five years, and responded eagerly when he asked me to write a foreword to *How Technical Analysis Works*. Bruce is one of those rare technical analysts who has been around many bull and bear markets across the trading and investing spectrum—from futures to equities to fixed income and foreign exchange.

For years the investing public and novice traders, as well as people in the industry, have needed a clear, concise book on technical analysis. Not a book to turn them into technical analysts, but a book that would really help them with their own or their clients' trading and investment strategies. This is that book.

Bruce not only has the experience, but as proven by this book, the ability to clearly convey information about the most important and most popular technical tools a trader or investor needs to know to be successful.

In this easy-to-use and enjoyable-to-read book, Bruce takes you through a step-by-step process, thoroughly describing why technical analysis is so valuable, and carefully explaining how to fully harness its potential.

In *How Technical Analysis Works*, you will progress from the history and logic of technical analysis through various kinds of charts, chart patterns, trends, trend lines, oscillators, and indicators. Bruce skillfully shows how each indicator works. And, equally important, when you should not use the indicator.

While the simple and clear explanations are unique features, *How Technical Analysis Works* also offers technical tricks, tips, and techniques—based on Bruce's quarter century of real world experience—that are unavailable elsewhere. Once you have finished absorbing these lessons, you will be armed with an array of weapons for trading and investing in today's markets.

How Technical Analysis Works levels the playing field between you and the professional trader.

Steve Nison, CMT
President—CANDLECHARTS.COM

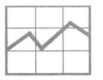

Introduction

You can learn about technical analysis in many ways. Countless books, magazines, seminars, newsletters, Web sites, and professional courses, as well as a few colleges and universities all provide information about the subject. After nearly 30 years of learning about and using technical analysis, I have come to consider it part art and part science. Actually, I prefer to call technical analysis a craft. I learned the craft of technical analysis over many years. I began by taking classes at the New York Institute of Finance with Ralph Acampora and then with Alan Shaw, both of whom shared their years of experience unselfishly. I also read books and attended seminars on technical analysis.

If you want to become a full-time technical analyst, one of the best ways to learn the craft is on the job, though that luxury is afforded to only a few people lucky enough to fall into such a position. I began to learn about technical analysis on the job at a commodity forecasting firm during the early 1970s, when it seemed as if everything soared in price—wheat, coffee, silver, gold, soybeans, and sugar, to name a few. I was exposed to many bull and bear moves, gaining a lifetime of market experience in just three years. Too many people jump into investing or trading with little understanding and no experience of at least one market cycle. The 1970s afforded me the great opportunity to track the rise and fall of many markets, to see how events in the news affected the markets, and, more important, to see how the markets responded to the news.

While on-the-job training, whereby you can learn from other people's mistakes and get paid to do something you love to do, may be preferable, such opportunities are few and far between. Absent on-the-job training, most often we turn to classes, books, or seminars.

Since the early 1960s, the number of different investment instruments has multiplied. Currencies now float, and interest rates can fluctuate sharply. Money moves around the globe easily and around the clock. We don't wait for chart books to come in the mail; we don't even have the patience to download a file from the Internet. Thousands of people are using technical analysis in some form, but most likely without a good framework in the basics, without a true understanding of what they are doing.

How Technical Analysis Works offers a tested approach to technical analysis. The book is organized in an order that builds comprehension and skills in a logical way to make it easy to understand the subject. My goal in writing was to provide investors, traders, and students with a good first book on technical analysis prepared for the twenty-first century.

Regardless of your level of experience and investment knowledge, this is a book you will keep and refer to for years to come. *How Technical Analysis Works* is the one book that tells you what is important, the book that shows you how technical analysis can be a timing tool, a selection tool, and, most important, a risk management tool.

The importance of using technical analysis as a risk management tool can't be stressed enough. Reduced to the basics, there are really just five possible outcomes from investing or trading—a large loss, a small loss, flat or unchanged, a small gain, or a large gain. The small gains and small losses will cancel themselves out along with the trades that are "scratches," or unchanged. Of the five outcomes, if the application of technical analysis can help you avoid large losses, then we are left with the very desirable outcome of large gains. That is what we are all looking for.

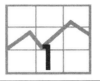

History and Background

Knowing something about the 120-year history of technical analysis in the United States can help you understand how these tools were developed and how they are best used. For example, it is not just a bit of trivia to know that a particular technical tool was developed in the late 1960s and early 1970s, when the stock market was in a broad sideways trading range. It explains why the tool does not work well in a strong uptrend such as the one we witnessed in the 1990s.

THE EARLY YEARS

People have remembered prices since the beginning of commerce. Remembering prices is just the start of the logic behind technical analysis. The prices of goods and raw commodities—silk, spices, gold, rice, horses, cattle—have been followed for centuries. People remembered the prices of last season, the extreme highs and lows, and more. For centuries, farmers have had a vital interest in following prices; the result of a whole season of sweat and toil will come down to the price they are able to get in the marketplace. If your livelihood depends on being paid for one crop of tobacco, coffee, or rice, you will have a strong interest in its price.

Technical analysis as we know it today dates back to the beginnings of organized exchanges. The New York Stock Exchange was established on May 17, 1792, when 24 brokers formed the first organized stock market in New York. As traders came together in one place and there was price discovery, people began to follow the prices of securities. In the very beginning, only those people at or near the exchange or involved in the securities business were able to follow prices. Market data was not collected and disseminated cheaply and quickly, as it is today.

It was not until 1867 that stock tickers were first introduced. Eventually, as prices at the stock exchange were disseminated over a paper tape to a wider audience, people began to follow prices more closely. Perhaps an early unnamed "tape reader" began to remember prices and volume and to notice patterns. The relaying of orders and market information took another leap forward at the end of 1878, when the first telephones were installed on the trading floor. Today, detailed market information is spread freely and quickly over the Internet.

Technical analysis developed from the repeated observation of market phenomena over time. A stock would hold at a particular price (support), then rally and subsequently fail (resistance) at some other price level. Think about a card player who is skilled at bridge, poker, or blackjack because of a good visual memory. Just as knowing which cards have come before can give you an edge in figuring out what card might come next, the tape reader gains a sense of a stock's price action and of what might come next. We don't know exactly what will come next (until we draw the very last card) but we can, through observation and experience, identify the more profitable patterns or setups, both in card games and in the securities markets.

Before the days of modern accounting, quarterly announcements, and annual reports, the best and certainly the most up-to-date information on the prospects for a company was its stock price. Even with all the media attention and rapid dissemination of news today, the price action of a stock is still the best and most up-to-date source for information on the company's prospects, including investors' hopes, fears, and expectations.

Tape watching is technical analysis in its most basic form. It is simple observation: watching stock purchases transaction by transaction; watching volume expand on a breakout to a new high and diminish on the eventual retracement. Observing these events and noting the outcome is no different from looking at a chart for an ascending triangle formation in an uptrend and anticipating a breakout to the upside. Storing these lessons away in the brain, seeing them repeat, and then reacting to them almost instinctively is what traders have always done. Eventually, traders and analysts became used to looking at price graphs instead of memorizing the patterns of individual trades. The graphs gave them the ability to form an opinion about any stock, commodity, or bond without following it in real time. Pick up a chart of anything; look at six or nine months of history and you can quickly see if it is going up, down, or sideways. You can quickly develop an opinion—bullish, bearish, or neutral—depending on the chart picture.

THE GROWTH YEARS: 1880 TO 1950

In the United States, it was not until the 1880s and 1890s that people began to put their ideas about price movements and market observations on paper. By the turn of the century, a few people began publishing their ideas and observations, and some of these ideas still work today, after decades of exposure—like the Dow Theory.

DOW THEORY

Dow Theory is widely known as a market forecasting tool, but it began as a method to describe the general state of business conditions. Charles Henry Dow, the first editor of the *Wall Street Journal*, wrote down his observations on the economy and business in the form of editorials, which were published in the *Wall Street Journal* between 1900 and 1902. Dow used the movement of stock prices as a barometer of underlying business conditions rather than as a tool to forecast stock prices.

Charles Dow published the first stock market average on July 3, 1884, consisting of 11 stocks, of which 9 were "rails." The rails were the Internet stocks of the 1880s. They rose and sank like dot-coms, and their industry, too, was transforming the United States. The average was split into industrials and rails in 1897. Dow Theory is the oldest and probably the most publicized method of identifying major trends in the stock market.

With the upsurge in short-term trading and interest in the over-the-counter market, or NASDAQ, in recent years, the ranks of followers of the Dow Theory have shrunk to a small handful of devotees. Many people believe the Dow now represents the lagging old economy and not the hot, new technology economy. Dow Theory has also been criticized for being late on turning points.

While Dow Theory may be widely recognized by name, only a fraction of the investing public could actually explain it and apply it today. Today, investors want instant analysis from programmed software. Application of the Dow Theory takes some experience, interpretation, and analysis. Dow Theory is useless to the day trader, to the person chasing a hot IPO, or to someone buying stocks on split announcements. With the stock market rising for nearly a decade with only relatively shallow dips, some people ask, why would anyone waste time trying to figure out a market timing approach from the last century?

CHARTS

It might make logical sense that line charts would have been the first charting method. Line charts can compress long periods of time and are the easiest to construct with just one data point per time period; but they do not seem to have been the first stock charts published. Point-and-figure charts, or what was known as the book method (because it was written down in a book), appeared in the 1890s. Charles Dow supposedly recorded stock prices in what he called the book method or figure charts, writing down the actual stock figures: $27, $28, $29, then a dip to $28, and so forth. *The Game in Wall Street and How to Play It Successfully*, published in 1898, by an anonymous author using the name of Hoyle was the first book on point-and-figure charting. Victor deVilliers published *The Point-and-Figure Method of Anticipating Stock Price Movement* in 1933, the first definitive work on point-and-figure charting. De Villiers changed Dow's charts by using Xs instead of the numbers representing the stock price.

For the majority of their history, point-and-figure charts were maintained by hand. Companies near Wall Street sent clerks or messengers to the offices of Morgan, Rogers, and Roberts in lower Manhattan to pick up the printed sheets that showed all the intraday movements. The most junior member of the technical department usually got the job of plotting all the reversals by hand on special chart paper held in large ring binders. Today, you may still find some clerks on the floors of the commodity exchanges keeping up point-and-figure charts on the particular markets they are trading, and the technical analysis department at Salomon Smith Barney still maintains charts by hand. However, this charting approach is now largely done electronically.

The origin of line charts is unclear, but bar charts seem to have come into use in the early 1900s; illustrations of bar charts can be found in publications from 1910. Bar charting appears to have become popular in the 1910s and 1920s.

EARLY INDICATORS

Indicators such as the timeless advance–decline line (A/D line) originated in the 1920s and 1930s. Credit for an early measure of business confidence and for the A/D line goes to Colonel Leonard P. Ayers. Colonel Ayers ran a company called Standard Statistics that was merged into a company headed by Henry Poor, and the new entity became Standard and Poor's in 1941. The Barron's Confidence Index dates back to at least 1932 and was first used as an indicator of general business sentiment. In 1959 a young technical analyst by the name of Joseph Granville showed how it could be used as a stock market timing tool, and I developed a use for it as a bond market timing tool in the 1980s. The Barron's Confidence Index can be found every week in *Barron's*, in the Market Laboratory Section.

It is interesting to note that books on fundamental security analysis came on the scene only after the Securities Act of 1933 and the Securities Exchange Act of 1934. *Security Analysis* by Graham and Dodd did not appear until 1934—an interesting factoid that every technician should remember. Richard W. Schabacker was perhaps the first person to use the words triangle, pennant, and head and shoulders to describe chart formations. His book, *Stock Market Profits*, was published in 1934 and has recently been updated and reprinted. Schabacker was the financial editor of *Forbes* magazine and authored two other books on the market, *Stock Market Theory and Practice* in 1930 and *Technical Analysis and Market Profits*.

In the late 1930s and for much of the 1940s there seems to have been a void in literature and new tools to analyze the stock market. Considering the economic and business climate of that time, that should be no surprise. Edwards and Magee saw their first edition of *Technical Analysis of Stock Trends* roll off the presses in 1948. This book was the bible of technical analysis for many years.

THE MODERN ERA

As data became readily available and analysts became comfortable with mathematical methods to explain and describe price action, the course of technical analysis took a dramatic turn.

In the late 1950s, a technician with a great mind and lots of promise, Joseph Granville, started to work at E. F. Hutton. In 1959, he published a short article on the Barron's Confidence Index in *Barron's*. He followed that initial article with two books that covered on-balance volume, the 200-day moving average, and other tools and concepts still very much in use today. Other great technicians who contributed to the craft of analysis over the years (but whose voices have been lost in our attraction to software) are Kenneth Ward, E. S. C. Coppock, D. G. Worden, Garfield Drew, and George Lindsay.

The 1960s saw tools like the Rate of Change (ROC), better known today as momentum, come to the fore along with the first use of the fund of funds concept. Jerry Tsai and others rose to prominence as aggressive stock traders who traded stocks with the help of technical analysis. The 1970s brought more math and new tools like the Relative Strength Index (RSI) developed by J. Welles Wilder Jr. Various moving averages dominated commodity trend-following systems. Richard Donchian popularized the 10-day and 20-day moving averages as well as the 4-week rule.

With the return of options, people like Marty Zwieg researched the put–call ratio. At the end of the 1970s, people like Fred Hitschler and Gerald Appel presented their work on moving-average envelopes, moving-average crossovers, momentum studies, and the Moving-Average Convergence/Divergence (MACD) oscillator.

The 1980s saw efforts at optimizing—taking the data and beating it till it yielded the results you wanted—or more politely, looking backward over some time period to see what worked in the past. After you optimized your technical study, you assumed that prices would behave in a similar manner in the future. This was a great approach if it worked, but you were simply in possession of the best backward-looking fitted moving averages. Why did technicians go through this process? It comes down to two reasons. First, they had these new tools called computers. Second, they had enough clean, post–World War II data to analyze and a burning desire to find the Holy Grail of investing and trading.

Those of us who live in the United States, with Wall Street as the center of the financial universe, tend to assume that technical analysis started in America. However, Japanese candlestick charts date back to the mid-1700s. Because the writings and technical tools from Japan were obscured from the West until the late 1980s, candlestick charts are not part of the U.S. history of technical analysis. In the 1990s, Japanese candlestick charts were offered on every major on-line charting service and from all the data vendors. Eventually, the charts could be seen on every day trader's screen. It is not difficult to get a computer to recognize candlestick patterns with a simple program, and now quantitative analysts use them to prove that technical analysis can work to the satisfaction of the academic community.

We are now into the twenty-first century, and technical analysis is buzzing with Artificial Intelligence and nonlinear approaches. Looking ahead, the sky is the limit for on-line indicators. As exchanges, especially commodity exchanges, go electronic, a network of Internet portals with price information, open interest, and volume data is likely to be developed, and technical traders will find it easier to analyze this information.

Technical analysis has always adapted to its environment, and I am certain that the bright young minds of today and tomorrow will find new and faster ways to look at the information emanating from the exchanges—even electronic ones. The recognition of patterns will be computerized and what was once subjective will be quantified and analyzed to death. If we keep in mind that trends move in cycles, it's reasonable to expect that someday people will probably return to the basics. We might even chart stocks by hand once again.

How Technical Analysis Differs from Fundamental Analysis

The two basic techniques for forecasting price movement are fundamental analysis and technical analysis. Many people are purists and follow only one technique, but many more traders and investors combine these two approaches in various ways. You will have to decide for yourself how you want to approach the markets and what methods you are most comfortable with. Some of the best traders use fundamental analysis to figure out the general direction of the market they are interested in, and then turn to technical analysis to time the entry and exit of their trades or investments. I have grown comfortable with my own particular approach, but that does not mean it will work for you. You need to study and experiment to find the approach that best suits your level of knowledge, the time you have available to do analysis, and your personality.

Obviously, in this book I make the case for technical analysis; but that does not suggest you should ignore other approaches—they all bring something to the table. Remember that no investment approach is perfect or flawless, and what works in one environment does not always work in another. There is no answer as to which approach is better, so keep an open mind.

THE FUNDAMENTAL APPROACH

Investors who use fundamental analysis watch the various economic factors that affect supply and demand as they try to forecast prices and find profitable investments. One of the principles that the fundamental analyst operates on is that any economic factor that decreases the supply or increases the demand for a financial instrument or a commodity tends to raise prices. The opposite is also in operation; that is, any factor that increases the supply or decreases the demand for a financial instrument or a commodity tends to lower prices. A fundamentalist forecasts stock prices on the basis of economic, sector, industry, and company statistics and data. The principal factors that affect decisions are earnings and dividends. The fundamentalist makes a judgment of the stock's value within some sort of risk–return framework. The stock's valuation is influenced by the economic environment.

THE GENERAL ECONOMY

Forecasting the general economic environment can become very complex for the fundamental analyst who must simultaneously evaluate economic factors, political forces, and even investor attitudes. If we take a closer look at just one fundamental indicator, you will understand how complex this can be.

Leading economic indicators can give investors good signals about the economic state for months ahead—the direction of interest rates and the direction of stock prices. The index of Leading Economic Indicators (LEI) includes 11 components, from the average workweek of production workers in manufacturing to the number of new building permits issued and the total money supply. That is what goes into just one fundamental indicator. To try to forecast each of the inputs and to do it right is a full-time job.

No one indicator dominates, and as business moves through an economic cycle, sometimes the market concentrates on some indicators and ignores others for a time. This adds another dimension to the job of the fundamental analyst, as he or she must also identify the factor that is currently of most concern to the market. Sometimes it is the employment situation, sometimes inflation or productivity. Each cycle is different.

THE TECHNICAL APPROACH

Technical traders or technicians believe it's simply impossible to sufficiently understand every factor that could affect supply and demand. Even if you could properly follow a host of factors, it is easy to overlook something that could substantially affect the market. There are factors we cannot quantify easily, such as political factors. From time to time there are sociological factors and psychological factors, such as riots, Watergate, Iran-contra-gate, Monica-gate, and terrorism, that can affect investor confidence.

Technical factors also surround and affect the markets. By technical factors we mean price, volume, and, in the case of futures and option markets, open interest, which is the number of futures or options contracts that remain open. These statistics are produced by the marketplace and are the numbers with which technical analysts are concerned. Technicians prefer to study past price movement and history to anticipate future price action. Technicians use indicators to determine the state of the market and to time investments. Instead of studying a host of economic indicators and company statistics to determine the possible price movement, the technical analyst looks at the price action of the market; that is the latest and best information about the market.

DIFFERENCES

The technician does not consider value in the sense in which the fundamental analyst uses the term. When fundamental analysts find a stock they like and it goes down, they like it more. It's on sale. When technical analysts find a stock they like and it goes up, they like it more.

There are other differences between technical and fundamental analysis that you will learn from experience. Fundamental news comes out slowly. This timing affects your decisions at both market tops and market bottoms. At a market bottom, your opinions about an investment are shaped slowly as you follow the news about a company, its products and sales and so forth. There is no harm in developing good, sound research on a company to ascertain its prospects. That approach is fine, as stocks and markets often take a considerable time to establish a base and begin an uptrend. Unfortunately, at a market top, changes occur more quickly. When a stock declines from a top, it typically falls much faster than its ascent. If you wait for the news on the company to unfold and turn negative, prices will often be a long way down from their best levels. Just remember that good news about a company always comes out faster than bad news.

THE LOGIC OF THE TECHNICAL APPROACH

Three basic assumptions support the technical approach to market analysis. Let us take a look at the basic assumptions before we actually study the methods.

THE MARKET DISCOUNTS EVERYTHING

The first assumption is that market action or prices discount everything. Said another way, the markets are barometers rather than thermometers. Markets are forward-looking. One of the oldest sayings on Wall Street is, "Buy the rumor and sell the news." This simple phrase symbolizes the discounting mechanism. Perhaps just as old is the saying, "The news follows the tape." Think about it. Have you ever bought a stock when "business couldn't be better," only to see it go down? The other extreme also works. The phrase "It's always darkest before the dawn" could be applied to Wall Street in that the best bargains are often available just when things couldn't get worse. The phrase "when there is blood in the streets" refers to times when things are at their worst. This is when markets hit bottom.

Traders and investors are motivated by information that is available to them, whether published or not. People also act upon changes in their expectations of events. Hopes, fears, needs, and even financial resources affect buying and selling decisions. Technical analysts have come to accept and assume that all the factors that could affect prices are already reflected in the price now. The markets are forward-looking by six to nine months. We act on what we believe the future will bring, not on today's news or the company's past laurels.

IS THE NEWS IMPORTANT?

A technical analyst might be interested in the news, but is really not concerned about why prices go up or down. Don't get me wrong. How a market trades in reaction to news can be very helpful information. A market that doesn't go down on bearish news has already discounted the news and is looking ahead to something else. Likewise, a market that doesn't go up on bullish news is in trouble—all the good news is out—and prices have begun to discount some adjustment ahead. Because people act on financial information that is not yet published, the market discounts the future.

In making a case for the point-and-figure method of charting in his 1933 book, Victor deVilliers put the discounting function this way: "The method takes for granted that the price of a stock at any given time is its correct valuation up to the instant of purchase and sales (a) by the consensus of opinion [*sic*] of all buyers and sellers in the world and (b) by the verdict of all the forces governing the laws of supply and demand."

PRICES MOVE IN TRENDS

The second basic assumption underlying the technical approach is that prices move in trends. Before these trends are established, technicians believe markets go through a period of accumulation, making a base before an uptrend is established; and a period of distribution, marking a top before declining. Trends can and do last for long periods of time. Have you ever noticed the long-term chart of the Dow-Jones Industrial Average that is shown in every piece of literature by the mutual fund industry? Some members of the academic community, as well as others, still argue that prices are random and that the study of price movement is fruitless. They believe that the markets are efficient and that investors behave in a rational manner. Some markets are fairly efficient and respond to new information almost immediately, but many markets exhibit prices that do not respond immediately to new information. Also, many people who are involved in the markets do not behave in a rational manner. Both of these facts fly in the face of the efficient-market hypothesis.

HISTORY REPEATS ITSELF

The third assumption made by technicians is that history tends to repeat itself. This assumption is based on the understanding that human nature has remained unchanged through the years. Greed and fear are two basic human emotions, and they have been found to live at market tops and bottoms ever since the very first open-air market took shape. I can't imagine a situation in which these two innate emotions don't exist after a prolonged rise or a long decline. At tops, nobody is left to buy after everyone has become convinced that the market will keep rising. At bottoms, nobody is left to sell; all the discouraged longs have finally sold out their positions.

THE RELATIVITY OF MARKET MOVEMENTS

Technicians have observed that market movements usually have a relationship to one another. Small consolidations or sideways moves whereby investors don't have as much time to accumulate or distribute shares are usually followed by short-term moves, and larger consolidations often produce larger moves. When a stock or other instrument has been through a major downtrend, a longer base-building period is normally required before the stock has the ability to mount a new sustained advance. It takes time to repair the damage, and time for the fundamentals to correct themselves, if possible. A small downtrend normally requires only a smaller and shorter rebasing period to start a new leg up. When viewed from the top, the old saying comes to mind: The bigger the top, the longer the drop.

FOLLOW THE SMART MONEY

The longer a market has been trading sideways at a high level, the more likely it is that the ownership of stock has moved from strong hands to weak hands. Farsighted investors may have purchased shares in the company years ago at a much lower price level, and are now realizing their gains and selling out to eager traders and new investors who believe that prices could go significantly higher. After all, the belief that still bigger price gains are possible will prompt investors to purchase a stock that has already seen a big markup.

"Strong hands or smart money" is a Wall Street expression that is often used but rarely defined in an intelligent and useful way. Imagine a group of shrewd investors who understand the economy or an industry, sector, or company inside and out, every nuance. They know when the price of the stock is below what it is really worth, or when prices are temporarily depressed, or when the company is going to be able to improve its fortunes. These "strong hands or smart money" investors buy the stock because of the strong underlying fundamentals. If the price of the stock dips slightly, they are not unnerved because they know nothing has changed fundamentally. They can endure temporary swings that make other investors nervous. Their knowledge makes them confident to hold the stock with strong hands—unshaken by minor dips.

The technical analysis of price movement provides a valid formula for successful investment decisions. So, with all the books on technical analysis and with all the Web sites that include charting software, why aren't people more successful? I think it comes down to execution and discipline. You need to learn to think for yourself. No book can do that for you, but the suggestions in Chapters 18 and 19 can help. Put them to work for you.

It's up to you. Do you want to follow old news to forecast prices, or do you want to use the latest prices to forecast subsequent prices? You can look at every fundamental input to deduce a forecast, or you can look at just one thing—price. Analysis of the market can be approached from either direction, but there is no reason why these approaches can't work together.

Major moves in the marketplace must be caused by an underlying change in the fundamentals, so technicians have something to learn from an awareness of the long-term fundamentals. By the same token, fundamental analysts can use charts and technical analysis to alert them that something may be shifting before the fundamental change has become clear.

The Role of Charts
in Technical Analysis

There are many types of charts and graphs, from simple to complex. In this chapter we will show you the most common charts that you can access at Web sites or from software packages. You should find most of these charts available as part of your on-line brokerage account. For competitive reasons, every on-line brokerage account offers bar charts and line charts or variations called mountain charts or dot charts. Many brokerage firms offer candlestick charts as well. A few might offer point-and-figure charts. The charts are also easy enough to maintain by hand if you have a small list of stocks. Even in this age of computers, many traders maintain a chart or two by hand to get a "good feel for the market," or because the data is not available in an inexpensive and easy-to-access database.

A CHART IS YOUR ROAD MAP

Over the years, traders have created many kinds of charts, driven by their desire to follow the market and influenced by their creativity and the tools at hand. Typically, the only limiting factors have been the availability of data and the number of hours in a day. No matter what your level of experience, charts should always be the first working tool of the technical analyst and the trader or investor. Charts give you a quick and concise history of the price action, which is something you should know before you trade. The fundamental analyst could even use long-term charts to quickly show the periods of major price moves, to identify key price-determining factors.

Several approaches to charting have developed over the years and each method has its own features, benefits, and drawbacks. At the very least, think of the chart as a road map of where you have been. In a fraction of a second, you can see the range of trading for the past year in a much more revealing way than looking at the figures in the newspaper that show the high and low for the last twelve months. At a glance, you can see if the trend is up, down, or neutral. It may take a leap of faith to accept the chart as a tool that can forecast where you are going. You will gain that confidence and faith by reading this book and by applying the techniques described here. *Just remember: A chart is only as good as its data and the experience you bring to reading it.*

TWO METHODS OF SCALING CHARTS

There are two methods of scaling the various kinds of charts you can work with—arithmetic or logarithmic price scales. Both of these methods are important and it is good to know when and why each should be used. More comprehensive Web sites and better software packages permit both scaling methods.

ARITHMETIC SCALING

The majority of charts you will encounter will be displayed on an arithmetic scale, which plots the units of measure using the same vertical distance. The distance between 1 and 2 will be the same as the distance between 11 and 12 or 21 and 22. The scale that runs up the right or left side of the arithmetic chart is designed to encompass a particular range. This method of plotting prices is fine in most instances, but long-term movements tend to need adjustment. See Figure 3.1.

Figure 3.1: Intel Trading History Using an Arithmetic Scale

Intel Corp (Nasdaq NM)   34.55   -0.099   -0.288%
D: 01/01/92   O: 1.52   H: 1.97   L: 1.48   C: 1.87   Y: 84.86

Prophet Financial Systems, Inc. (*www.prophetfinance.com*) Used by permission.

This chart shows ten years worth of trading history of Intel (symbol INTC), one of the 30 stocks that currently make up the DJIA. It uses an arithmetic scale. Notice how the price action from 1992 to 1995 is compressed. Three uptrend lines are needed to show the multiyear advance.

LOGARITHMIC SCALING

Logarithmic (also known as log or ratio scale) charts are often used for a quick check of relative performance as well as long-term trend analysis. Securities, indexes, or averages that are plotted on a logarithmic or ratio scale use identical vertical distances on the chart to show identical percentage moves. If your charting package does not offer logarithmic charts and you want to draw them by hand, these charts need their own special graph paper (available in office supply stores). A number of

Web sites offer the ability to display information in either type of scale. The Web site may offer only a scant 5 or 10 years of data, but the ratio presentation might show some interesting relationships for some of the recent high-flying technology issues. Too many of these stocks soared from their initial public offering (IPO) prices to the hundreds of dollars and back down again in 2000 and 2001. Looking at the moves as percentages may put them in perspective.

Think about the movement of the Dow-Jones Industrial Average (DJIA) over the past 70 years. Today, a move of 100 Dow points in a day seems like a normal fluctuation. With the DJIA

Figure 3.2: Intel Trading History Using a Logarithmic Scale

Intel Corp (Nasdaq NM)   34.55   -0.099   -0.288%
D: 01/01/92   O: 1.52   H: 1.97   L: 1.48   C: 1.87   Y: 103.52

Prophet Financial Systems, Inc. (www.prophetfinance.com) Used by permission.

Here we see 10 years worth of trading on Intel on a logarithmic scale. On this chart, the dramatic rally during 1992 to 1995 is not compressed as in Figure 3.1. Another major percentage change advance occurs in 1995 and 1996 and can be seen clearly on this display. One uptrend line can be fitted here, identifying the major trend for this market leader.

over 10,000, a 100-point swing is only 1%. In the early 1930s, when the DJIA was on its way down from around 300 to around 40 or 50 points, a 10-point swing could have been a 20% or 25% move.

Because of the higher levels of the popular stock market averages today compared to only 20 years ago, movements in the major averages are now displayed in points and in percentage changes by the media. Dealing in percentage changes also makes it easier to understand swings in the foreign markets, especially something like a 300-point move in Japan's Nikkei 225 average, which recently stood in the 10,000 to 15,000 area.

Another key characteristic of logarithmic charts is that intermediate and long-term trend lines are rarely penetrated unless a trend reversal of more than just passing significance is developing. This idea can be seen clearly in Figure 3.2.

DEPENDABLE LINE CHARTS

The simplest chart to construct and maintain is the line chart or its identical twin, the close-only chart. Line charts are very easy to construct and still have a place among today's more sophisticated approaches. You probably see line charts every single day in newspapers and magazines and on television and don't give them much thought. Next time you look at the front page of the *Wall Street Journal* or the *Financial Times* or *Investors Business Daily* or read an article on finance in a business magazine, slow down and look more closely. On any given day the editors will use a line chart to show the latest economic data series or the price chart of a stock, the euro, or bond yields. The media are well aware that a picture or a chart is worth a thousand words and that a chart can display data and show trends more quickly than several paragraphs of text. An example of a daily line chart is shown in Figure 3.3, and a weekly line chart is shown in Figure 3.4. Both charts quickly show you the direction of prices without much detail.

Figure 3.3: DJIA 30 3-Month Daily Line Chart

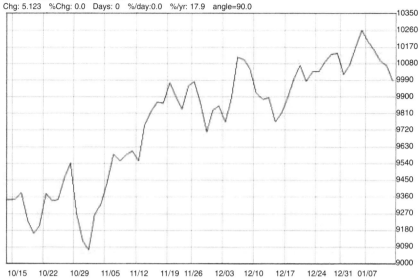

Prophet Financial Systems, Inc. (www.prophetfinance.com) Used by permission.

This daily line chart of the DJIA quickly shows the direction of prices from the middle of October 2001 into January 2002.

Figure 3.4: DJIA 30 Four-Year Weekly Line Chart

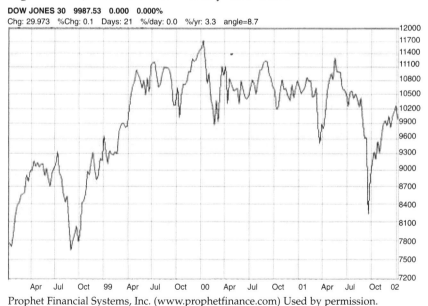

Prophet Financial Systems, Inc. (www.prophetfinance.com) Used by permission.

Four years of weekly price data are shown in this line chart. The 1998–99 advance is seen clearly before the market enters the sideways or neutral trend for much of 2000–01.

Constructing Line Charts

A line chart has prices or data on the vertical or *y* axis and a time measure on the horizontal or *x* axis. Plotting the price or other value and joining all the plots together with a line is how you construct a line chart.

Imagine you were given a table of five years of monthly data on housing starts. You are looking at 60 data points. While they may be neatly arranged in rows and columns, can you figure out the trend of the data? Are the numbers rising or falling? It is very difficult to discern a trend by just looking at the numbers, but if you plotted the data you should be able to notice any trends. A line chart can transform a table of data to a clear visual representation so one can quickly find a pattern or trend in the numbers. It is equally probable that prices or data are not showing any trend, but are fluctuating sideways.

Line charts are best used to track a single statistic, which can be a price, an economic release, or even temperature readings. The statistic could be a daily price "fixing" for a cash commodity such as gold or a currency, or a weekly data point such as API crude oil stocks or unemployment claims. Even a monthly economic release such as housing starts or industrial production can be quickly displayed with a line chart. If available, volume can be shown along the bottom and moving averages of a price can be added, too. Trend lines can be drawn to illustrate and identify the trend as well as reversals, which are discussed in Chapter 4. Line charts are often found in nonbusiness periodicals and can quickly show a trend that would be hard to discern from a table of data.

The identical twin of a line chart is a close-only chart. The close-only chart plots only one observation per period—the close—even though more data is known. Indeed, we may know the open, high, and low prices for the period, but by displaying only the closing price or settlement price we can produce a cleaner-looking chart to highlight the trend. Figure 3.5 shows a monthly close-only or line chart.

Figure 3.5: DJIA 30 15-Year Monthly Close-Only Chart

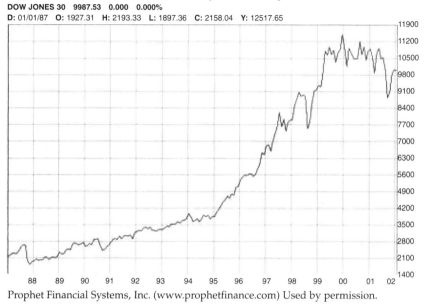

DOW JONES 30   9987.53   0.000   0.000%
D: 01/01/87   O: 1927.31   H: 2193.33   L: 1897.36   C: 2158.04   Y: 12517.65

Prophet Financial Systems, Inc. (www.prophetfinance.com) Used by permission.

This is an example of a monthly close-only or line chart. The hugh bull market of the 1980s and 1990s is displayed clearly on one chart. Clarity is one of the key features of the close-only or line chart. This chart of the DJIA clearly shows the major rise in share prices in the late 1980s and the rapid rise of the 1990s. Showing the highs and lows would detract from the clean visual presentation.

BENEFITS OF LINE CHARTS

A simple line chart can serve a very real purpose in this age of sophistication by showing a lot of history in a small space. A 15-year line chart (like the one in Figure 3.5) shows the trend of the security or index much more clearly than a 15-year bar chart that includes the high and low in addition to the close. Over longer periods of time, the intraday fluctuations mean less than the overall trend. Trying to see every jiggle could make you lose the so-called big picture. Using a line chart makes a lot of sense for industry, sector, or group work when one is more concerned with the relative strength of the sector or group than with the daily or weekly changes. We discuss relative strength in detail in Chapter 12.

DRAWBACKS OF LINE CHARTS

The main drawback to line charts is that they delete potentially important price information. The extreme high and low made during any time period is important to know when calculating key percentage retracements. The key 50% retracement, like all retracements, is calculated from the extreme peak to the nadir, and some accuracy is lost if you use only the closing price. The extreme high or low made in the past week could be used for the placement of a buy or sell stop level, just as you could use the extreme of the last reaction high or low. Traders sometimes buy or add to positions when the stock makes a new high. You would not be able to use these techniques properly if you worked only with line charts.

BAR CHARTS

While a line chart requires only one data point per day (or week or month), a bar chart or vertical bar chart requires three pieces of information: the high of the period, the low of the period, and the close or settlement. (Open, high, low, and close charts are also widely available, but you need to know how the opening price was derived in order to know what value it has.)

CONSTRUCTING BAR CHARTS

In the bar chart or vertical bar chart, the horizontal or x axis is used to represent time, while the vertical or y axis displays the price. Below the x axis you can display the trading volume, open interest in the case of futures and options, or whatever indicator you select. The bar chart can display up to four pieces of information: the open, the highest price, the lowest price, and the closing price. The distance from the high to the low is shown as a solid bar and is called the range. The opening price or the first trade is shown as a tick or hash mark to the left of the bar. The closing price, settlement, or last trade is shown as a tick or hash mark to the right of the bar. A single bar is shown in Figure 3.6.

Figure 3.6: A Single Bar from a Bar Chart

A bar chart uses a vertical line to reflect the range (high and low) in a given time period. The left-sided notch on the vertical line represents the opening price, while the right-sided notch represents the close. This individual bar can depict time frames ranging from one minute to multi-year periods, but traders usually find bar charts useful for intraday, daily, weekly, and sometimes monthly tracking.

Sometimes an opening price is omitted from the chart, and if you are updating charts by hand from the data in the newspaper, you won't find the opening price shown unless you are plotting futures contracts.

In addition to the price information, bar charts usually display the number of shares or contracts traded, or what we refer

Figure 3.7: IBM 2-Year Weekly Bar Chart

Prophet Financial Systems, Inc. (www.prophetfinance.com) Used by permission.

This is a weekly bar chart of IBM covering a 2-year span in which the stock is stuck in a sideways or neutral trend, mostly between $132 and $84, but the highs and lows of the bar chart show the extremes reached.

Figure 3.8: A 2-Year Weekly Bar Chart of Agnico Eagle Mines with Volume

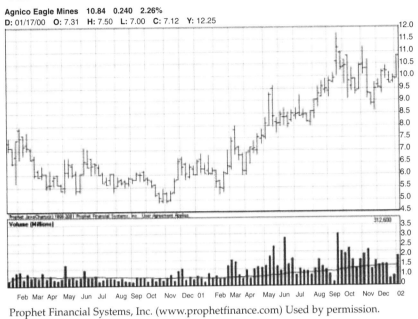

Prophet Financial Systems, Inc. (www.prophetfinance.com) Used by permission.

Here is a weekly bar chart with volume along the bottom of the graph. Notice how volume generally expands during the 2001 uptrend.

to as volume. This is normally shown as a histogram below the horizontal or *x* axis. A histogram plots the information as a vertical bar. In the case of volume, each day or week would be plotted as a vertical bar with a height that properly represents the period's volume. For the futures markets, most charting services also display the total open interest as a line chart overlaid in the area with the volume histogram. Open interest is the number of contracts that are held outstanding by the longs and shorts. Because there is a long for every short, the convention is that we only total one side of the open contracts. Open interest gives you information about the liquidity of the contract. Contract markets with low open interest should probably be avoided, because execution costs or slippage will most likely be higher. See Figures 3.7 and 3.8.

INTERPRETING BAR CHARTS

Let's examine a single, individual bar and see what information it reveals and how we can interpret it. As noted earlier, the opening price is not usually shown in the newspaper. Some charting software, on-line systems, and Web sites automatically create an opening price—a price they synthesize. A synthetic opening price is derived depending on the relationship of the prior day's close to the high–low range of the current day. As an example, if yesterday's close were within the range of the current day, the prior close would be used for the opening of the current day. If the previous close were above or below the current range, then the high or low of the current day would be used as the open. In markets that trade 24 hours a day, the opening price is meaningless, but some creative analysts and traders divide the day into three 8-hour periods, each with its own open and close.

The close or closing price is normally the last transaction of the session—when the closing bell is rung or the gavel is banged. In the futures market there is an official closing time, and a settlement price is determined to reflect the average of the prices during the close. For distant or thinly traded contracts, a settlement price might be established that is actually outside the range of traded prices. In this instance, the high or low would have to be adjusted to include or match the settlement.

The high price seen during the day represents the highest price paid for the security. The low price represents the lowest price paid for the security.

Much information can be gleaned by looking at today's closing price compared to yesterday's. You can quickly see who is the most anxious and who is in control—buyers or sellers. This is the relationship that is carried on the evening news reports and in print media the next day. "Dow Industrials plunge 300 points" means that the DJIA closed down 300 points from the prior day's closing price. A rise or fall in the market is good news or bad news depending on your existing position. If you are short or out of the market, then a 300-point decline is good; but if you are long in the market, a decline is bad. When you compare today's closing price to yesterday's, you can distill some rough guidelines about who appears to be driving the market.

If today's closing price is above yesterday's close, then we can assume that the buyers are more aggressive than the sellers and they have pushed the market up. If today's closing price is below yesterday's close, then the sellers were more aggressive. The farther away today's close is from yesterday's close, the more aggressive the buyers or sellers are. See Figures 3.9a and 3.9b.

Figure 3.9a: Bulls Maintaining Control

Figure 3.9b: Bears Maintaining Control

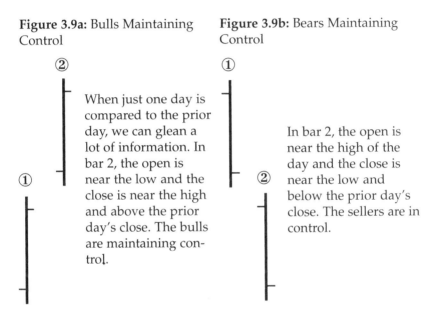

When just one day is compared to the prior day, we can glean a lot of information. In bar 2, the open is near the low and the close is near the high and above the prior day's close. The bulls are maintaining control.

In bar 2, the open is near the high of the day and the close is near the low and below the prior day's close. The sellers are in control.

In addition to looking at the close and its relationship to the range, we can look at the range to gain additional information. Let's start with the upside. If buyers are becoming aggressive, they will be very interested in buying and will bid a stock up even when it hits some selling pressure. Prices will move up quickly and the move will likely be significant. So, an expansion of the price range on the upside normally shows that the buyers are more aggressive or more committed. See Figure 3.10a.

The opposite is true for sellers. Sellers who have a sense of urgency to get out of long positions will drive prices down and down, despite buying support that may appear. See Figure 3.10b.

Figure 3.10a: Expanding Range of the Upside

Figure 3.10b: Expanding Range on the Downside

An expanding range on the upside shows that buyers are increasingly eager to buy the security. A contracting range on the upside shows that buyers are becoming less aggressive.

An expanding range on the downside shows that sellers are becoming more aggressive and eager. A contracting range on the downside shows that sellers are drawing back and are less eager.

When price ranges contract from their recent pattern, the controlling side, long or short, is losing commitment or urgency. The shrinking price range can mean that traders who have sizable positions and profits are reducing or lightening their positions. When they do so, a more balanced relationship exists between the bulls and bears. Contracting ranges can also indicate that when a market has risen, it may be viewed as expensive and sellers may be attracted; or if the market has fallen, it may be viewed as cheap and buyers may be attracted. Thus, contracting price ranges on the upside indicate that the buyers are becoming less aggressive and less committed. Contracting price ranges on the downside reveal that sellers are less committed or are less eager to pressure prices lower.

A lot of information can be gleaned from just one bar, and still more from several bars and price patterns. Keep this in mind as you read Chapters 6, 7, and 8.

BENEFITS OF BAR CHARTS

Bar charts are very versatile. You will find them everywhere—from the financial sections of newspapers to Web sites, charting services, and printed chart books. A daily bar chart is usually the default chart that is called up when you check your portfolio on-line via your brokerage account. Bar charts can be constructed for any time frame, from very short-term intraday charts on out to yearly charts. You can add volume along the bottom of the chart and your favorite indicators, which are all driven by price and time—something you can't do with a point-and-figure chart. The data needed to construct a bar chart is readily available, and the chart is very easy to maintain by hand.

DRAWBACKS OF BAR CHARTS

Frankly, there are very few drawbacks to using bar charts as such. When you deal with very long-term trends, a bar chart can be a fuzzy-looking chart compared to a simple line chart, but in most instances this is not a debilitating handicap. The various patterns we present in the following chapters might be too subjective for some people to become comfortable with, but that is not a direct function of the chart itself. If you are looking for long-term price objectives, you might have to use a point-and-figure chart, but weekly and monthly bar charts will also show longer-term price objectives. Given their versatility and lack of drawbacks, it is no wonder bar charts are so widely used.

POINT-AND-FIGURE CHARTS

After line and bar charts, the next major charting technique you should know about is point-and-figure. This method of displaying price action may rank among the least popular and is one of the most misunderstood. Some knowledge of the approach is important from a historical perspective, but these charts are tools in your technical arsenal that can come in handy when analyzing a consolidation pattern or when trying to view a longer-term price objective.

Point-and-figure charting probably hit its low in popularity just about when on-line charting systems became available for intraday price analysis. Point-and-figure charts look at intraday price changes; a 60- or 30- or 15-minute bar chart does the same thing, but without the filtering effect of a point-and-figure chart, and with a time scale. A bar chart shows the whole range of trading for the time period, but a point-and-figure chart shows only price changes of a predetermined size. A point-and-figure chart showing only $1 movements will not show a high of $21.50. Only the last full-dollar trade, at $21, will be plotted, and thus some of the price action is filtered out. The security can trade actively between $21.00 and $21.99, but no entries are recorded until $22.00 is traded.

CONSTRUCTING POINT-AND-FIGURE CHARTS

On a point-and-figure chart, there is no obvious element of time and no illustration of volume. To construct a point-and-figure chart, a starting point must be decided. Time can be illustrated as a function of trades, but not by actual time moving along the bottom of the chart. We can show the first entry for Monday on the chart, but we don't show all of Monday's activity. In a 1-point, point-and-figure chart, a figure is not entered until the stock moves up or down one full point or more. A point is normally $1, and this is where the name of the chart comes from. See Figure 3.11.

Depending on the security, its volatility, and the time frame you want to operate with, the point size or the box size can be changed. The smaller the price increment, the more changes in direction that will be seen and thus the more sensitive the chart. A larger box size will make the chart less sensitive and more useful for long-term analysis.

The y or vertical axis shows price, but the x or horizontal axis can show time only in a rudimentary way. A bar chart moves over one bar to the right for every trading day or week, but a point-and-figure chart moves only when there is an entry. Depending on the size of the box and the reversal, the chart will move across the page slowly or quickly. To get a sense of time, one can replace an X with an M for the first trade on Monday for an active chart, or one could replace the X with a J for the first trade in January.

Besides entering a letter to denote the passing of time, another convention in constructing point-and-figure charts is

Figure 3.11: A Point-and-Figure Chart of IBM

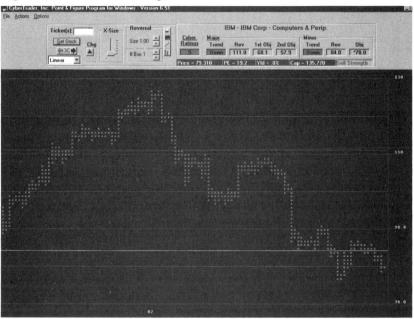

Courtesy of Cyber Trader, A Charles Schwab Company.

This is a one-box reversal chart. The dates added along the bottom vary in length. Notice that there was more price activity in 2000 than during 2001. The measuring technique of the count is also illustrated with an upside price projection.

using 5 and 0 when the stock trades at 5, 15, and 25 and at 10, 20, 30 and so forth.

THE WHEELAN METHOD VERSUS THE COHEN METHOD

There are two schools of thought regarding the construction of point-and-figure charts: the Wheelan Method and the method developed by Abe W. Cohen.

The Wheelan Method uses intraday price reversals to create the basic one-unit or box chart. This is the technique used by Charles Dow and de Villiers, and is the one described earlier and shown in Figure 3.11. The point-and-figure approach popular-

Figure 3.11A: Point-and-Figure Reversal Chart of IBM

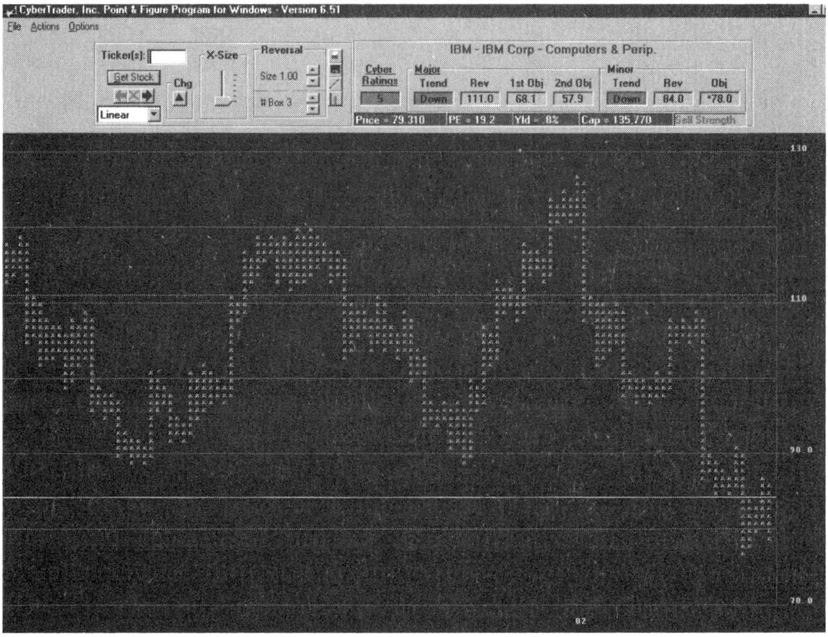

Here are some of the classic top and bottom formations associated with the Wheelan method of maintaining point and figure charts.

ized by Abe Cohen in 1947 is known as the 3-box reversal method and is a kind of shorthand or condensation of the Wheelan Method. The 3-box method seen in Figure 3.11a uses a 3-box reversal, which means the price must reverse by an amount equal to or exceeding three boxes from the most recent high or low extreme of the last column before a new column can begin. Looking at the market swings in the 1940s, Cohen reasoned that there weren't many 3-box reversals in a day, so it wouldn't be necessary to look at intraday data. Thus, one big advantage of the Cohen method is that you use only the high and low prices, which are easily found in the newspapers or on various Web sites.

Figure 3.12 shows some of the classic top and bottom formations associated with the Wheelan method of maintaining point-and-figure charts.

Figure 3.12: Point-and-Figure Reversal Patterns

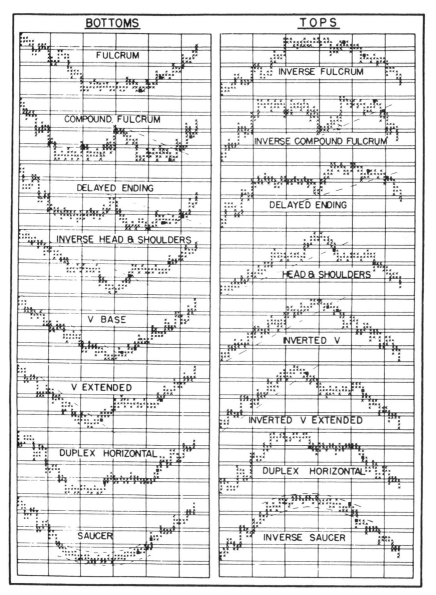

Here are some of the classic top and bottom formations associated with the Wheelan method of maintaining point-and-figure charts.

BENEFITS OF POINT-AND-FIGURE CHARTS

Point-and-figure charts are adaptable and can fit the needs of many different traders and investors by varying the sizes of the box and the reversal. Small box sizes and reversals can be used for short-term traders and larger boxes for investors looking for long-term moves. Buy and sell signals become clear on point-and-figure charts when you look for breakouts and breakdowns.

Adding trend lines, a point-and-figure chart can give you more precise trading signals. While bar chart patterns do yield price objectives, broad sideways patterns on point-and-figure charts can give you an indication of some longer-term price objectives not available with other approaches.

DRAWBACKS OF POINT-AND-FIGURE CHARTS

A sense of time and of volume are both missing on a point-and-figure chart, which is among the drawbacks of this method. Volume is the second key item to come out of the marketplace after price, and not having volume on the chart could present a problem. For example, we can clearly see a breakout on the chart, but we have no idea whether volume has expanded to confirm the move. We could just follow the price action and use appropriate money management, but all the same, knowing that the breakout was occurring on strong volume would give you more confidence in buying. Other charting methods put the volume right below the chart, making it easy to combine the information.

"Timing is everything." That's a glib phrase used by traders, but it does warrant some attention. Having a sense for when a market may break out is important. Point-and-figure charts are not time-dependent and the price patterns are not necessarily symmetrical, which is one way to get a sense of timing. The longer-term price objectives we get from a point-and-figure chart are nice, but we have no indication about when they may be reached. When Charles Dow was updating his point-and-figure charts over 100 years ago, perhaps time was not as important; but with today's lightning-speed moves in the marketplace, time is very important. Another drawback of point-and-figure charts is that if you have to produce or update them by hand, you will find it very time-consuming.

CANDLESTICK CHARTS

The last major charting approach we discuss happens to be the oldest, and is very popular today—candlestick charting. The candlestick methods used today were developed in Japan from writings in the 1700s. The approach appears to have grown out of the trading of rice on the Dojima Rice Exchange in Osaka, Japan.

Candlestick charts are similar to bar charts. Both use the vertical axis to represent price and the horizontal axis to indicate time. Both use the high, low, and close, but candlesticks also include the open. In fact, the relationship of the open to the close is key with this method.

CONSTRUCTING CANDLESTICK CHARTS

Candlesticks show the open, close, high, and low on a vertical line with a box called the "real body." The combination of shape, color, and position relative to the other candlesticks creates patterns. Candlesticks are more colorful than line charts, bar charts, or point-and-figure charts, literally and figuratively. Many of the candlestick patterns actually look like candles with wicks. You have the same vertical high–low bar of the Western bar chart, but you add a rectangular-shaped box between the opening and closing prices. This rectangular area is left open or unshaded or white if the close is higher than the opening. If the close is below the opening, the rectangular area is shaded or darkened. The open box is bullish—we closed higher than we opened. This is saying that on a short-term basis, the trend is up. The darkened box is quickly seen as bearish because the close is lower than the opening. The area between the open and the close is called the real body, while the ranges above and below the real bodies are called the upper and lower shadows. Figure 3.13 shows how the candlesticks are created.

Figure 3.13: Constructing the Candlesticks

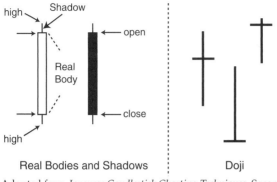

Real Bodies and Shadows | Doji

Adapted from *Japanese Candlestick Charting Techniques,* Second Edition. (c) 2001 by Steve Nison. Used by permission from Prentice Hall Press.

On the left we see two candle formations. The first one is open or empty and indicates that the close is higher than the open. Here the bulls are in charge. In the next bar the close is below the open and the bar or real body is black. Here the bears are in control. On the right side of the illustration are three examples of when the open and the close were the same price. This pattern is called a *doji* and shows a balance between the bulls and the bears.

CREATE YOUR OWN CANDLE LINES

Take a piece of graph paper and cover up the right side of Figure 3.14. Look at the information given on the left side of the figure. Draw short horizontal lines for the opens and closes and then extend the vertical bar up and down for the range. Then outline the area around the open and close. Draw the candle lines for each of the five sessions. Then uncover the right side of the figure and compare your work.

BENEFITS OF CANDLESTICK CHARTS

Why have candlesticks become so popular? Several answers come to mind, and they focus on the benefits of candlesticks. Candlestick patterns focus mostly on reversals; because of that, they are quicker to identify turning points in that the various candlestick patterns take only one, two, or three bars to form. Traders are always looking for something to get them ahead of

Figure 3.14: Drawing the Candle Lines

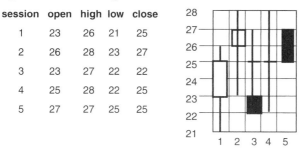

session	open	high	low	close
1	23	26	21	25
2	26	28	23	27
3	23	27	22	22
4	25	28	22	25
5	27	27	25	25

Here is a quick exercise in drawing the individual candle bars. See directions on page 38.

everyone else, and the speed of the candle patterns has attracted the interest of thousands of short-term traders.

Candlesticks can be combined with all Western techniques, so you aren't left with an either-or choice. You can combine candles with trend lines, moving averages, oscillators, retracements, volume, and open interest, or even with the Elliott Wave approach. While a head-and-shoulders pattern on a bar chart might sound interesting the first few times you hear it, the candles have more colorful names like tweezer bottoms and tops, upside gap two crows, rickshaw man, spinning top, and many others. The names of the various bar chart patterns only describe the shape of the pattern, such as a rectangle. The candlestick patterns give you a clear idea of whether the pattern is bullish or bearish. Where would you expect to find an evening star pattern? At a top, of course. A morning star sounds and is bullish.

Another good feature of the candle chart is that the picture jumps out at you; it's not like a flat-looking line chart or bar chart. Also, candle patterns are less subjective than other methods. In fact, some Web sites and software programs have been programmed to find these patterns, but they don't yet have everything programmed. So far, programmers are having a hard time defining a trend, a trading range, and other factors crucial to using candlesticks effectively. A lot of the effectiveness of the candlestick patterns depends on their location and the trend preceding the pattern, as well as your experience in their interpretation. See Figure 3.15.

Figure 3.15: Microsoft Daily Candle Chart—Patterns Need Interpretation

Microsoft Corp (Nasdaq NM) 68.61 -0.669 -0.966%
D: 08/09/01 D: 64.98 H: 65.55 L: 64.30 C: 65.01 Y: 69.34

Prophet Financial Systems, Inc. (www.prophetfinance.com) Used by permission.

Here are two similar candle patterns known as a hammer. One is during the week of September 10 and one is during the week of September 24. They look similar, but only the second one is followed by a white or bullish candle and generates a reversal.

DRAWBACKS OF CANDLESTICK CHARTS

There are a few drawbacks to candlestick charts. The first problem is that the candle charts do not provide any price projections. You get a reversal pattern, but then how far are we going? You will have to use other techniques to determine that. Another problem is that there are very few continuation patterns. Continuation patterns give you confirmation that the up- or downtrend is still in force and provide you with confirming price targets as well as low-risk entry points.

It is questionable whether candlesticks were meant to be used on intraday work. The key relationship between the open and the close needs a true opening, whereby people have a chance to react to all the overnight news and respond in the morning. What does the open mean on a 60-minute candle chart? What makes it different from the close of the previous 60-minute candle? Nevertheless, a lot of people have found that intraday candle charts are effective. I even use them to time the entry of my trades, but I find it difficult to show how the logic can be applied intraday.

OTHER CHARTING TECHNIQUES

Other charting techniques have been used with varying success by the public. There are other Japanese charting methods like the 3-line break method, *kagi* charts, and *renko* charts. There are Equivolume charts and Gann charts and swing charts. You might find these methods useful, so I won't discourage you from finding out more about them; but if you do, you will find your-self moving further away from what most investors are familiar with. If you use these charts in a public forum or in an Internet chat room, you will need to take time to explain how they are constructed. Unlike a simple math equation, charts and patterns and indicators need to be explained to most people.

HOW TO DECIDE WHICH CHART TO USE

After investors have become familiar with basic charting tech-niques, the most common question is, "What kind of chart should I use?" This question is difficult to answer because one must know and understand the objectives of the users, the mar-kets they want to be involved in, their time horizon, and their risk parameters.

We know that some charts have advantages over others and that some may not be effective for intraday use, but all charts are equally valid. First, you need to decide what time frame you want to operate in.

WHAT IS YOUR TIME HORIZON?

For day trading, you need to look at charts that can show the activity of less than a day. These could be 1-minute bar charts, tick charts, 15-minute candlestick charts, or a sensitive point-and-figure chart. If you trade in the time frame of days to weeks, you should look at daily bar charts, daily candlestick charts, and 1-unit point-and-figure charts in the style of Wheelan. If you try to position stocks or other instruments for several weeks to perhaps six or more months, then you should use weekly bar and candle charts, and less sensitive point-and-figure charts, or the 3-box method by Cohen. And last, but not least, if you buy and hold for a year or longer, then you should be looking at monthly or maybe even quarterly charts.

Even if you are a longer-term investor who uses weekly and monthly charts, you can still look at daily charts for the timing of your investments. Just because you anticipate that an investment will be held for two or three years because of the underlying fundamentals, that doesn't mean you should ignore buying near the bottom of a base pattern or close to a long-term moving average or near a major trend line.

WHAT ARE YOUR NEEDS?

You must think about what information you need to enter and exit the market. For instance, if I am a trader with a weekly time frame, but I am trying to enter a volatile market, I may need to look at intraday charts to improve the timing of my entry. If you lean on the fundamentals for your ideas and then go to the charts for the execution, your needs may focus more on identifying support and resistance areas from point-and-figure charts, so you can buy near support or sell near resistance.

A COMBINATION CAN BE THE KEY TO SUCCESS

Knowing that each charting technique has its own strengths and weaknesses, a combination of charts and time frames could be what you need to accomplish your goals. In deciding on an investment, you might start with 5-year or 10-year line or bar charts to get a good idea of the long-term trend and the price extremes.

Is the stock we are looking to buy closer to a 5-year low or high? If we look to hold this investment for several months, then a look at a weekly chart going back three years will help in positioning the stock. Use this time frame to look at the retracements the stock makes. Have they been deep or shallow? How long have they tended to last? This information will be important to know when you go to the daily bar or candle chart to finally execute the trade.

On the daily bar chart, we may be looking for a simple key reversal to buy, or we may do the same on a candle chart. The potential price target will influence what you risk on the trade, and this is when you might consult a point-and-figure chart for longer-term price objectives.

Trend lines on a bar chart, candle chart, or point-and-figure chart could be used for entry points. Go long when the trend line is successfully tested. A break of a key trend line could be used as an exit signal.

The best advice is to look at as many charts and time frames as you can. They all represent important price action and should only add clarity to your thinking. Getting confirmation of the trend, a price target, or a support or resistance level from another chart will only build your confidence in going forward with the trade or investment.

Keep Your Eye
on the Trend

Trends are basic to technical analysis. The fact that prices move in trends is one of the assumptions of technical analysis, as we discussed in Chapter 2. When you look at price charts closely, you can often see prices moving along an imaginary straight line. Trends are a basic starting point to analyze securities, but some traders and analysts say it is all you really need to know. Others, like Jack Schwager, who has written extensively about technical analysis and is perhaps best known for his interviews of very successful traders, think the importance of trend lines is overrated and that they are often drawn in hindsight. Nevertheless, it is rare that there is an important change in price trend that is not accompanied by the breaking of a trend line. That is reason enough to pay attention to trend lines.

People who are new to technical analysis often ask me what is the one best system to follow. I always answer that it is to learn to identify trends and to draw and use trend lines. Often the conversation turns to, "Is it a good time to buy or sell?" or "What do you like here?" If you also have these questions, you will learn to answer most of them for yourself once you learn to read the trends in the marketplace.

TYPES OF TRENDS

A simple definition of trends is a good place to start. An uptrend is a series or succession of higher highs and higher lows. A downtrend is a series or succession of lower highs and lower lows, and a sideways or neutral trend has equal highs and lows. See Figures 4.1, 4.2, and 4.3.

45

Figure 4.1: A 5-Year Weekly Bar Chart with Uptrend Line

Marsh & Mclennan Cos Inc 103.80 -0.469 -0.450%
D: 01/13/97 O: 34.81 H: 35.52 L: 34.32 C: 35.43 Y: 148.00

A 2-year uptrend is clearly shown here on Marsh & McLennan, with higher low and higher highs being made.

Figure 4.2: A 5-Year Weekly Bar Chart with Downtrend Line

Freept-mcmo Copper & Gold Cl B 13.69 0.090 0.662%
D: 01/13/97 O: 29.87 H: 32.13 L: 29.25 C: 31.62 Y: 30.54

This chart of Freeport-McMoRan Copper & Gold, Inc. shows the pattern of lower highs and lower lows remaining intact as the downtrend line defines the erosion in this stock.

Figure 4.3: A 5-Year Weekly Bar Chart with Sideways or Neutral Trend

Asa Ltd 20.95 −0.059 -0.285%
D: 01/13/97 **O:** 35.00 **H:** 35.13 **L:** 34.00 **C:** 34.50 **Y:** 39.09

Prophet Financial Systems, Inc. (www.prophetfinance.com) Used by permission.

Gold stocks have been out of favor for years, and the sideways trend of ASA Ltd. shows the stock with a neutral trend, stuck between $14 and $23 for three years.

About 70 years ago, Robert Rhea took the ideas of Charles H. Dow and turned them into a clear definition of a trend:

> Successive rallies penetrating preceding high points, with ensuing declines terminating above preceding low points, offer a bullish indication. Conversely, failure of rallies to penetrate previous high points, with ensuing declines carrying below former low points, is bearish.

IDENTIFYING TRENDS

In application, there are two methods for identifying trends: a short-term method using highs and lows, and a longer-term method using peaks and troughs. At a minimum, for an uptrend, you need a bar with a higher high and a higher low than the previous bar, or a bar that makes a high above a peak after a higher trough. See Figure 4.4.

Figure 4.4: Illustration Showing Simple Definition of an Uptrend

Figure 4.5: Illustration Showing Simple Definition of a Downtrend

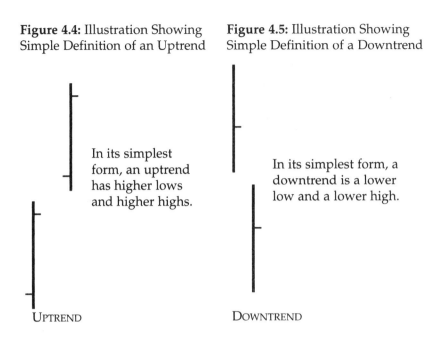

In its simplest form, an uptrend has higher lows and higher highs.

In its simplest form, a downtrend is a lower low and a lower high.

UPTREND

DOWNTREND

The minimum requirement for a downtrend is a bar with a lower low and a lower high than the previous bar, or a bar that makes a low below a trough after a lower peak. A lower low and lower high are shown in Figure 4.5.

When you see higher lows or higher troughs, don't make the mistake of believing you are seeing an uptrend.

A neutral or sideways trend is shown in Figure 4.6.

Figure 4.6: Illustration of a Neutral or Sideways Trend

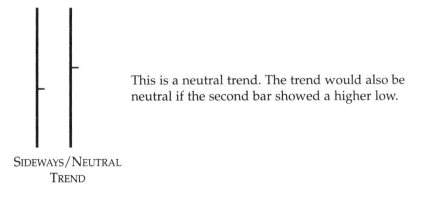

This is a neutral trend. The trend would also be neutral if the second bar showed a higher low.

SIDEWAYS/NEUTRAL TREND

Let's imagine you do excellent fundamental research and you find a company, companies, or sectors you want to invest in. What next? As a technician, you should look at a chart. By looking at whether the trend is up, down, or sideways, you can quickly see if anyone else finds your stock picks attractive. If the stock is in a downtrend, your thinking could be early, you could be missing something, or you could even be wrong.

To some degree, the correct or proper placing of a trend line is often more art than science. Trend lines describe the speed of price change in trends. They do not define trends as such. You will develop your own special technique for drawing trend lines, built on your past experiences in other markets or past cycles. Like an auto mechanic who looks at a bolt and instantly knows whether the size is $5/16$ or $13/16$ or $15/16$, by looking at enough charts you will eventually get the knack of reading and seeing trends quickly and effortlessly.

There are various types of market participants who each trade or invest in different time frames. Some people are day traders; some people operate in terms of weeks, and others in months or even years. All of these participants will be looking for trends to develop in the time frame they operate in for trading. Regardless of what time frame you decide to operate in, analysis should always begin with the longest time frame chart available, and then you can drill down to the time frame being traded.

HOW TRENDS ARE FORMED

Sometime during high school or college you may have been exposed to the law of inertia: *An object in motion will continue in motion in the same direction until it meets an opposing force.* The same is true of trends. In an uptrend, investors will tend to resist paying more for a stock than the price that others have recently paid unless the stock keeps going up, giving the person hope or confidence that it will continue to gain. In a downtrend, people will resist selling a stock for less than the price that other people have been getting unless the price keeps sliding and fear builds that it will continue to skid.

Imagine for a moment that you are a key employee of the Acme Company, or a competitor or someone in the neighboring community. The Acme Company comes out with a new product and business is good. If you are a shareholder, you will not sell your shares because the company is doing so well. You may become a buyer of the stock because you see that business is good. By not selling or by becoming a buyer, you are keeping shares off the market or you are reducing the available supply. With the supply of available stock reduced, there is a tendency for the stock to rise. At some point, news of the company's success spreads to the brokerage community, other investors, and perhaps a wider reach of people in this particular industry. The price rises as people buy, and the rising price attracts more attention as the general public notices.

As the supply becomes reduced, new buyers must increase the price they are willing to pay to acquire the shares they want. This is the rationale underlying an uptrend.

WHY UPTRENDS END

Why do uptrends end? At some point the market has discounted the good news about the company. The price of the stock has risen to reflect the company's improved outlook. An announcement or earnings report may come out and some traders may sell on the news. If there is a sharp price rally leading up to the news announcement, you might expect many traders to take their profits.

A downtrend may even develop. Some investors may decide the rise has gone too far, and the price of the stock starts to decline because they stop buying at these lofty levels. They may even become sellers. Another possibility is that early sales and earnings estimates may prove to have been too optimistic, and the reality and disappointment may bring more sellers to take their profits. This is not hard to imagine if you have been watching the business news during the past year or two. Others who may have bought near the top of the advance may sell, taking a loss, to avoid even a bigger loss. All of these different sellers keep the decline going and create a downtrend.

DRAWING TREND LINES

Trend lines can be drawn in two ways. The first way to draw a trend line is to connect the tops or highs or peaks in the case of a downtrend, or to connect the bottoms or lows for an uptrend. As few as three points are needed to draw a trend line, with each point marking the top or bottom of a move or "wave."

It is important to realize that trend lines can and should be redrawn in the course of a cycle. They should not be static tools and should not be drawn in hindsight. Trend lines can go from the extreme low or high or from the penultimate low—the lowest point of the down leg that was completed just before the final bottom was made. (Here closing prices are not used, but the daily-low ranges.) See Figures 4.7, 4.8, and 4.9.

Figure 4.7: A 5-Year Weekly Bar Chart with Uptrend Line

Oceaneering 20.60 -0.749 -3.50%
D: 01/13/97 O: 17.87 H: 18.12 L: 17.00 C: 17.12 Y: 29.14

Prophet Financial Systems, Inc. (www.prophetfinance.com) Used by permission.

Here we see a 3-year uptrend line drawn through the lows. The uptrend line through the lows is broken, but the stock rallies again.

Figure 4.8: A 3-Year Weekly Log Chart with a Redrawn Downtrend Line

Textron is in a clear downtrend, with volume expanding on the declines and lessening on the rallies. The stock breaks one downtrend line, but the new low in late 2001 allows the redrawing of another line.

Figure 4.9: A 3-Year Weekly Bar Chart with Uptrend Lines

This chart of Conagra uses the penultimate low (the next-to-the-last bottom) and the first new high to produce a predicted trend line. Another uptrend line can be drawn parallel to the first trend line.

Figure 4.11: A 10-Year Log Chart

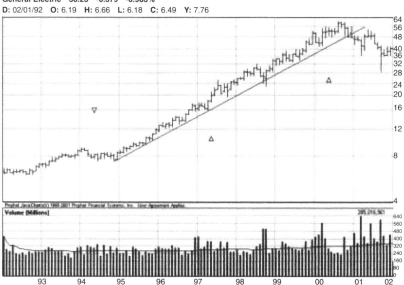

General Electric 38.23 -0.379 -0.983%
D: 02/01/92 O: 6.19 H: 6.66 L: 6.18 C: 6.49 Y: 7.76

Prophet Financial Systems, Inc. (www.prophetfinance.com) Used by permission.

Market bellwether General Electric maintains a 6-year uptrend line on this log chart. Notice how volume expands with the advance, confirming the move.

Figure 4.12: A Daily Bar Chart with Volume

Textron Inc 41.25 -2.16 -4.99%
D: 07/31/01 O: 55.40 H: 55.42 L: 54.50 C: 54.79 Y: 56.33

Prophet Financial Systems, Inc. (www.prophetfinance.com) Used by permission.

Notice on this daily bar chart of Textron that the stock goes up $12 from the low, but the volume does not improve on the rally and the stock quickly sinks from $44.

TIME HORIZONS

Trends can also be described in terms of time. The labels may vary, but generally short-term trends last days to perhaps weeks; intermediate-term trends last weeks to months; and long-term or major trends last months to years.

Futures traders may use the same terminology but shorten the time spans. For a futures trader, short-term means hours to days; intermediate-term means days to weeks; and long-term generally means three to nine months.

When you draw trend lines, consider the time horizon. On a very short-term intraday chart, you should accept the bare minimum in looking for a trend. You cannot look for uptrends or downtrends and make several tests to confirm the trend; there just isn't enough time to allow for that when the trend may only last until midday or early afternoon. Trends develop on daily, weekly, and monthly charts, and the breaking of these longer and longer trends takes on more and more significance.

TREND LINES AND VOLUME

Volume is a confirming tool to the technical analyst. The significance of a trend line is determined by the number of points connected at tops or bottoms, the length of time the trend is in place, and the expansion of volume (if known) along the trend. As a stock rises and pulls back to an uptrend line, the ideal pattern you want to see is volume expanding on the rally up away from the trend line, and then volume slackening or drying up as the price pulls back toward the trend line. Expanding volume on the rally tells you that more and more people are convinced of the rise in prices and more shares are being accumulated. Lighter volume on the pullbacks tells you that the buyers are for the most part hanging on to their positions and not dumping their recent purchases. See Figures 4.11 and 4.12.

Figure 4.11: A 10-Year Log Chart

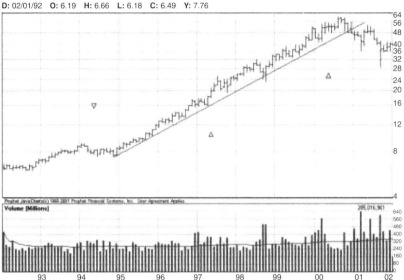

Market bellwether General Electric maintains a 6-year uptrend line on this log chart. Notice how volume expands with the advance, confirming the move.

Figure 4.12: A Daily Bar Chart with Volume

Notice on this daily bar chart of Textron that the stock goes up $12 from the low, but the volume does not improve on the rally and the stock quickly sinks from $44.

TREND LINE BREAKS

Let's assume you have a long position in XYZ; you bought it at $15 after a retracement to $10 from $20, and it recently moved up past $20, establishing a new high and reconfirming the uptrend. You decide to draw a line connecting the lows at $5 and $10 (the higher low). The stock trades higher in steps, rallying, consolidating, and rallying. When it reaches $45, a broader consolidation begins; the stock trades sideways till it reaches the uptrend line drawn from $5 and $10. The stock breaks or trades below this line intraday, but manages to close back above it. What do you do?

Breaks of trend lines are perhaps the hardest to use for buy and sell signals, because they can add more subjectivity to a technique that is already subjective. When you add in false breaks, the issue is even more of a potential problem.

I think intraday breaks of trend lines are the hardest signals to deal with because of the human factor and the time factor. If you have a long position and the stock, bond, or commodity has dropped a few cents or points through the trend line you have drawn covering the last six months, you are thrust into the position of making a decision to sell. Time is working against you because the close is approaching minute by minute. It is your position, and, more important, it is your trend line. The ticking clock adds to the pressure to make a decision now. You cannot easily ask someone else for a second opinion and hope they can draw the exact same trend line to confirm your thinking. The pressure is solely on you. Do you become frozen and hope that the stock will trade back up above the trend line? Or do you take action, selling out at the market?

You want all your trades and investments to be winners, and so you look at the market and the quote for the stock again and again, trying to gain the courage to convince yourself it is a weak quote and the stock is likely to go even lower, so that you can finally accept the decision you are about to make. You don't know what the future will bring, but you must make a reasoned decision now.

What you must understand is that investing or trading is all about cutting losses. You need to avoid the large loss that depletes your capital. You need to have a stake to come back again tomorrow. There will always be other opportunities; you must have risk capital to invest.

In grappling with the problem of exiting a position with an intraday break, analysts and traders naturally invented other signals. The first exit or entry rule for trend lines is the 1% rule. The rule is very simple to calculate and apply. If the security trades more than 1% below the uptrend line, you sell. This is a mechanical signal; at 1% down you get out, with no second-guessing.

For some people, the 1% rule was too tight and seemed to give some false signals in that the stock quickly traded back up above the trend line. So a wider 3% rule was used. A 3% intraday break of a rising or falling trend line has come to be accepted as one of the ways to respond to trend line breaks.

Intraday breaks of 1% or 3% did not satisfy everyone, so analysts moved toward using the close as the signal—one or more closes below the trend line or over it. Using a closing price creates new problems. You need to wait for the close to get a signal, and for the most part you have to wait until the next open to act on the signal. This delay to the close and the next opening can adversely affect your trading results if the stock is moving fast and sharp.

That's the bad news. The good news is that if the intraday dip below the trend line was temporary, the stock might have rallied before the close. Waiting for the close and making a decision overnight can also be good in that it won't interfere with your day job; you can reflect on your investment and act calmly in the morning with an order to liquidate. See Figure 4.13.

Another variation of a signal is to wait for two closes below the trend line. Similar to the situation in which you move from 1% to 3% on intraday breaks, moving from one close to two closes below the trend line can reduce the number of false signals, but it can expose you to more risk until you liquidate the position.

Figure 4.13: A Daily Bar Chart with Broken Uptrend Line

Pride International(delaware)   12.63   -1.01   -7.46%
D: 07/13/01   O: 15.60   H: 15.92   L: 14.90   C: 15.01   Y: 17.18

Prophet Financial Systems, Inc. (www.prophetfinance.com) Used by permission.

Pride International has a nice rally for three months, but in January the stock closes below the uptrend line. That is your signal to get out.

RETURN MOVES

Adding to the problem of spotting and acting on signals from trend line breaks is the return rally and failure. Sometimes when a stock breaks below an uptrend line it continues to decline, and you know that the drawing and interpretation of the trend line was correct. At other times a stock may make a shallow break of the trend line and then rally to new highs. If this happens and you think the stock still has more upside potential, you can repurchase the stock when the new uptrend is established. Finally, a stock may make a shallow dip and then rally back to the underside of the uptrend line, where the stock subsequently fails and turns down again. While this kind of price action can put you on an emotional roller coaster, it does show you that other people are acting on the trend line you have drawn.

TREND LINES THROUGH THE CLOSES

Now you have learned the typical way to draw trend lines and get signals from them. Let's look at another approach you might try before becoming too committed to using the extreme highs or lows. As I mentioned earlier, trend lines can also be drawn through key closes. Using the closes brings up an interesting discussion: How important is any one price during the trading day? Is the extreme high or low more important than the close, or even than the opening price?

Keeping in mind that the markets are always discounting everything we currently know about a company or commodity as well as about the future, the close becomes not just the last price at 2:30 P.M. or 3:00 P.M. or 4:00 P.M. Rather, it is the sum total of what people believe that security is worth that day.

A trading day has its own rhythm and pace. People watch the evening news on television and in the morning they read the newspapers, with analysis and reports from the prior day. Some people react to the news and want to buy or sell early in the day, generally near the opening. This dates back to days before price information was readily available over the Internet. Before you could click on a Web site or watch the stock market ticker tape along the bottom of the television screen, you had to call your broker to get intraday prices.

While the public has a long history of buying early in the day, the closing price was and probably still is the price most watched by the public. The print media has something to do with this. *Investors Business Daily*, for example, shows the closing price followed by the net change for the day in its stock tables. Over on the right is the day's high and low. We have learned to read from left to right, and the close is the first thing we see in the papers.

The close is where the short-term professional trader gets out of positions rather than holding positions overnight. The close or settlement price is the one securities and commodities accounts are valued at and the one margin calls are typically based on, as well as the key input for most-trend following technical trading systems employing moving averages.

There is an old saying that only fools or liars sell the high and buy the low. A professional on the floor may be able to do it, but we normally don't get that "edge." In securities or commodities trading, "the edge" is an expression that refers to being able to buy on the bid side and sell on the offer side when you are a market-maker or part of the market on a trading floor.

When a market order to buy goes to a trading floor, it is executed at the best offering price—the lowest price at or above the market at which people are willing to sell. When a market order to sell arrives on the trading floor, it is executed at the best bid price—the highest price at or below the last price at which someone is willing to pay for that security.

Specialists, market-makers, independent floor traders, and speculators are there on the bid and offer sides of the market, providing liquidity to the market so orders can be executed quickly. Part of the value of their seat or membership is this "edge." For you or me to buy at the low price for the day, we would have to use a limit order and have someone else sell to us as the best bid.

The fact that it is difficult to buy the bottom or sell the top also means that a lot of the volume is not done at the extremes of the day, unless the market traded up or down and stayed there. The high is made when we run out of buyers and the low is made when we run out of sellers. For some markets, the opens are very busy with volume, and the orders reflect that in "market on open" orders. The close of the market or the last part of the trading day can also be very busy in terms of volume as various traders or institutions rush to get in or to get out.

That is why I prefer to draw my trend lines through the closes. Sometimes these trend lines can give you an early signal compared to trend lines drawn through the highs or lows. Sometimes the signals might be late and you will wish you hadn't waited for the close. Nothing is perfect and nothing is for sure, so you have to balance what is important to you. In practice, I would draw both types of trend lines. It takes only a few seconds to do and it might give you a fresh clue about the trend. See Figures 4.14 and 4.15.

Figure 4.14: A 10-Year Log Chart, Trend Line Drawn Through Closing Price

Disney (walt) Co. **21.87** **-0.419** **-1.87%**
D: 01/01/90 O: 9.24 H: 9.72 L: 8.37 C: 8.59 Y: 47.66

A favorite stock for many years, Disney penetrated the major uptrend line in late 1999, but did not close below it until late 2000. During 2001 the stock traded above the uptrend line from below, but never closed above it.

Figure 4.15: A 10-Year Log Chart, Trend Line Drawn Through Price Lows

Disney (walt) Co. **21.26** **-0.609** **-2.78%**
D: 12/01/92 O: 13.61 H: 14.93 L: 13.08 C: 14.19 Y: 46.40

In this example, the major uptrend line is drawn from the December 1991 low, and the sell signals would come in December 2000 on trading below the trend line, or not until the close below it in mid-2001.

INTERNAL TREND LINES

Internal trend lines are drawn through the price action instead of over or below it. Internal trend lines are most often found with hindsight. Despite that drawback, internal trend lines can be useful for short-term trading, as prices pass above and below the trend line. Figure 4.16 shows an internal trend line.

Figure 4.16: A Bar Chart with Internal Trend Line

Intl Paper   41.04   -0.439   -1.05%
D: 01/25/99   O: 41.38   H: 43.50   L: 39.50   C: 39.56   Y: 58.77

Prophet Financial Systems, Inc. (www.prophetfinance.com) Used by permission.

For over a year, International Paper traded back and forth around this internal trend line. Traders could have bought dips to the trend line and dips under the trend line. When the trend weakened, rallies to the underside of the trend line could have been sold.

Trend lines can appear as part of major tops and bottoms and as necklines or as a warning of a reversal. See Figure 4.17.

A few words of caution: Some people stop using trend lines when they latch onto other indicators, especially those easily created on a computer. These indicators are secondary tools and are *derived from* the price action, as opposed to actually *being* the price action. People see buy and sell signals displayed for them

Figure 4.17: A 4-Year Bar Chart

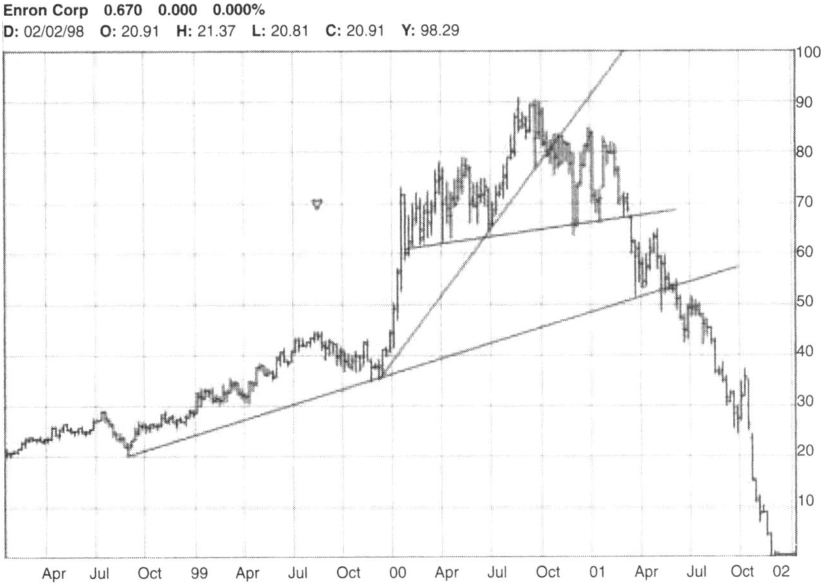

Enron Corp   0.670   0.000   0.000%
D: 02/02/98   O: 20.91   H: 21.37   L: 20.81   C: 20.91   Y: 98.29

Prophet Financial Systems, Inc. (www.prophetfinance.com) Used by permission.

Here is a stock that got a lot of attention during its rise and its fall. One uptrend was broken at $80, followed by the neckline of a top pattern (see Chapter 6) just below $70. You could still have sold at $50 when the 2-year trend was broken.

along the bottom of a chart, and some take them at face value instead of investigating further.

USING TREND LINES SUCCESSFULLY

To become adept at finding and using trend lines, you need to look at lots of historical charts. Just take a look back at the "fallen angels" of tech stocks from 1999, 2000, and 2001. Would a simple trend line have helped you get out of a technology or biotechnology stock that began a slide to the downside? You wouldn't have gotten out at the top, but you might have avoided a lot of pain and suffering by making a decision to sell instead of riding a stock back down. If your stock breaks a lengthy uptrend, you'll be unlikely to ignore it on a chart. See Figure 4.18.

Figure 4.18: A 10-Year Monthly Bar Chart

At&t Corp   19.11   0.210   1.11%
D: 02/01/92   O: 18.38   H: 19.18   L: 18.19   C: 18.38   Y: 58.38

Prophet Financial Systems, Inc. (www.prophetfinance.com) Used by permission.

This long-term chart of AT&T illustrates that you should not ignore the breaking of a major uptrend line, even when you see that the stock has major support under the market between $44 and $36.

When a stock is found tracking a particular trend line, it is likely (but not certainly) going to continue along that trend line. An investor or trader who can spot a trend gains a big edge in determining his or her strategy in the market. Always remember two things: First, trend lines are works in progress and they should be adjusted as the market shifts. Second, what makes trend lines significant is time and volume.

The Key Building Blocks of Support and Resistance

If the trend line is the first tool of the technical analyst, then the concept of support and resistance is the second most important tool to grasp (the type of chart technique notwithstanding) when learning about technical analysis. Like trend lines, support and resistance levels, or zones, also tend to be very subjective in their application and interpretation.

Support and resistance areas are key building blocks in chart reading, entering and exiting positions, and money management. Unfortunately, there are few hard-and-fast rules about support and resistance, especially in forecasting, where you expect to find resistance at an all-time high or support at an all-time low. In addition, you will need to learn to deal with ranges and bands or zones of support and resistance, instead of just one price level, if you want to be successful.

DEFINING SUPPORT AND RESISTANCE

Support is a level or area at which buyers overcome selling pressure. It is an area of price consolidation or congestion that is below the current price level of the security.

Resistance is a level or area at which sellers overcome buying pressure. It is an area of price activity above the security's current price level.

These levels or areas are not hard to find; most areas where a considerable amount of volume has traded could be noted as support or resistance levels. See Figures 5.1 and 5.2.

Figure 5.1: A 2-Year Weekly Bar Chart Showing How Support Becomes Resistance

Prophet Financial Systems, Inc. (www.prophetfinance.com) Used by permission.

Amazon, a one-time-popular, high-flying stock, found tremendous support at $60 for seven months. After the buying support gave way in April 2000, the $60 level became resistance.

Figure 5.2: A 1-Year Daily Bar Chart Showing Resistance

Prophet Financial Systems, Inc. (www.prophetfinance.com) Used by permission.

For nearly four months, the $17 to $18 area becomes clear resistance for Amazon. Every rally is met with sellers.

WHERE SUPPORT AND RESISTANCE LEVELS COME FROM

Support and resistance areas form because market participants remember price levels, and they tend to react as a group when a stock returns to those prices. A simple example will make the concept easy to understand. Let's imagine that you and other investors bought a stock at its initial public offering price of $20. People who did not buy the stock at the offering price are interested in buying it at that level, and they buy the stock at $20 or perhaps above $20 as interest in the stock builds. Other buyers come in and the stock trades up to $22.

The stock may trade back and forth between $20 and $22, but let's imagine that at some point the stock slips down to $16. Some traders will hold on to the stock, hoping that its fortunes will reverse and it will trade back above $22. But if the stock remains depressed, owners of the stock who bought it in the $20

Figure 5.3: A 1-Year Bar Chart Showing "Get Even" Point

El Paso Electric 14.20 0.050 0.353%
D: 01/12/01 O: 11.20 H: 12.29 L: 11.20 C: 11.56 Y: 16.50

Prophet Financial Systems, Inc. (www.prophetfinance.com) Used by permission.

El Paso Electric held support at $15 during June and part of July. When the stock slipped under $15 in late summer, all the rallies met with resistance. Holders of the stock were trying to "get even" at $15.

to $22 area will begin to think it would be nice just to break even. If the stock does trade back up, the desire to get out at break-even will become stronger and stronger as the stock approaches the $20 to $22 area.

To put this price zone into perspective, the more sideways trading that occurs, the greater the supply of stock will be. There will be more people who want to "get even," and therefore there will be more resistance to the stock's advance. See Figure 5.3.

Precision Doesn't Count

Support and resistance are not precise concepts. When support develops during a decline at a price short of the exact level, it is usually because traders are anxious. They remember the prior resistance level at $22, but they start buying on the way down at $22.75 and $22.50 because they are anxious or even fearful they will not have the opportunity to buy again at $22.

On a few occasions, eager traders might push a market too quickly through a support level, and support might not develop until just beyond the support area. Whether support is found short of the expected level or just beyond the level will tell you how eager or fearful traders are.

Resistance, like support, is also not an exact concept. Sometimes you will see resistance develop short of the exact expected level. This is because people may want to get out of losing positions before the exact level is reached, because they fear that the market may not get to that level or that it may not hold there for long. So traders may begin to sell at $19.50 and $19.75, before the market gets back to the $20 level.

Role Reversal

We have seen that when support is broken on the downside, it then becomes resistance. The opposite is also true; resistance, once broken, becomes support. This reversal of roles is due to the memory of traders and investors who want to get out of losing trades at break-even, and traders who want to increase winning positions by buying more stock at or near support.

This role reversal leads to the formation of trends, because in an uptrend, market pullbacks or reactions will tend to find

Figure 5.4: A 1-Year Bar Chart Showing Reversal of Support and Resistance

Intel Corp (Nasdaq NM)   34.55   0.000   0.000%
D: 01/17/01   O: 33.00   H: 33.06   L: 30.12   C: 30.50   Y: 35.57

Prophet Financial Systems, Inc. (www.prophetfinance.com) Used by permission.

Here Intel is stuck in a sideways trading range between $26 and $32. When the stock sinks under the September 11 decline, the subsequent rebound finds resistance at the former support level of $26. The resistance is eventually overcome, and then the top of the resistance becomes new support, back up at $32.

support at the last resistance level. In a downtrend, reactions or rallies will tend to find resistance at the last support level. This is shown in Figure 5.4.

DETERMINING THE VALIDITY OF SUPPORT AND RESISTANCE

All support and resistance levels are not equal. The strength of a support or resistance level depends on several factors, such as the number of times the level or area was tested, the volume of trades transacted there, how long ago the formation appeared, and whether it was a round number or a "big figure." Even knowing the type of security will help in determining the validity of the support or resistance area.

The more times a level or zone of prices is tested, the more important that level becomes. (This is similar to our discussion of trend lines in Chapter 4.) A level that is tested six times and holds tends to be more important than one that was tested only twice. The more times a support or resistance level is tested, the more traders will remember it and the more traders will be likely to be committed near it.

When a large volume of trading occurs in a support or resistance area, that adds to its validity because a greater number of traders and investors will remember the level, so their commitment to the level will likely be greater.

The further back in time the support or resistance area was formed, the dimmer the memory, and the more likely that people have already acted on new information and may not respond in the same way again. They moved on by liquidating their positions. An area of support or resistance that was formed recently tends to attract a greater number of people who are still committed to the level. Thus, these nearby levels have more validity or potency.

When a support or resistance level forms at a round number or a big figure, such as $100 or $1,000 or DJIA 10,000, many more people will remember the level because it is easy to remember and obvious. In turn, the more people who remember and act at that level, the stronger the support or resistance will be.

UNDERSTANDING PSYCHOLOGICAL SUPPORT OR RESISTANCE

Technical analysts also consider psychological support and resistance. It may be visible on a chart not because people are reacting, but because we are looking at an index (or an average) that may itself not be traded. The level works as an indicator even though the components may be moving in different directions.

For many years DJIA 1,000 was significant psychological resistance even though we did not actually trade the DJIA but only some of its components. (Think about a visible chart point like the DJIA 10,000. Years ago it was the DJIA 1,000 and, if Chuck Kadlec, author of the book *Dow 100,000*, is correct, it could someday be the DJIA 100,000.)

Psychological resistance is not the same as the psychological resistance at retail to paying $10 rather than $9.98 or $20 instead of $19.98. Indexes in the securities markets are composed of anywhere from 17 commodities or 30 stocks (in the case of the DJIA) to as many as 5,000 stocks (the Wilshire 5000). The stocks in the averages are added up and divided by the number of stocks to arrive at the average.

Since the advent of stock index futures in the early 1980s, actual support and resistance to any given index can be identified because you can buy and sell the underlying futures contract or Exchange Traded Fund (ETF) that shadows the actual cash index.

USING SUPPORT AND RESISTANCE

Support and resistance levels are useful for placing stops and can form a key part of your money management approach as well as helping you decide when to take profits. If a stock has just rallied from a consolidation area or support zone, this can become a good place to enter a long position because a protective sell stop can be placed just below the support area. If the stock falters and declines after your purchase, you would look to the support area to halt the decline. The stock might hold at or above the support area and eventually start to rally again, but if the stock continued to fall, the move through the support area would tell you the market has reversed and your losses must be cut short. See Figure 5.5.

On the upside, if you noticed a top pattern and wanted to short an issue, one of the places to enter would be at the under-

Figure 5.5: A 1-Year Bar Chart Showing Resistance from Old Support

Prophet Financial Systems, Inc. (www.prophetfinance.com) Used by permission.

This chart of AOL shows the stock finding support during July at $42, which was the old resistance in March. AOL rallies at the beginning of August and stops short of resistance, beginning at $48. AOL turns down to a new low, creating a downtrend. A rally from $39 fails at new resistance at $42, the intersection with the downtrend line.

side of a new resistance area. Ideally, you have tracked the stock closely and you are able to enter a short position as the stock breaks below a support level. Once the stock moves down, this prior support level becomes an area of resistance. Investors and traders who bought the stock will be anxious to get even if the stock rallies back. As the short seller, you would place your protective buy stop over the new resistance area.

If the stock overcomes the resistance and moves higher, you will know you were wrong and the breakdown was a false move. You could have had a very profitable short position, but the key to long-term success will be limiting your losses. The

Figure 5.6: A 6-Month Daily Bar Chart Showing a Zone of Support

Intl Business Machines   120.31   0.000   0.000%
D: 07/16/01   O: 108.53   H: 109.38   L: 107.28   C:107.82   Y: 129.64

Prophet Financial Systems, Inc. (www.prophetfinance.com) Used by permission.

IBM established a zone of support with the lower end at $111.11. The bottom of the support area is clear, and it can be used as a stop-loss point. If the stock trades back down under $111.11, you will know your assessment was wrong and take action to get out of any longs.

breaking of the resistance area is the market's way of telling you to cut and run. This is shown in Figure 5.6.

FINDING SUPPORT AND RESISTANCE

There are many ways to find resistance or to know where you might expect to find support. Besides reading a chart from right to left to see the last place the stock found support or resistance, you can also employ various tools like retracements, price objectives, moving averages, trend lines, and multiples of a key price low to anticipate support or resistance.

RETRACEMENTS

Retracements occur in the natural unfolding of uptrends and downtrends. Stocks can rally too fast and get caught by too much optimism and then profit taking, and pull back or retrace some of the prior rally. Stocks can also sink if the market becomes too pessimistic, and a rebound can occur, retracing part of the previous decline.

Consider a stock that makes a base at $20 and then quickly runs up from $20 to $40. At $40 there are many investors who have substantial profits on paper. Some investors may be sitting with a 100% return, and a number of these investors may be ready to take their paper profits and convert them into the real thing by selling. This selling tips the balance and the stock

Figure 5.7: A 3-Year Weekly Chart on a Log Scale Showing Retracement

Patterson-uti Energy Inc (Nasdaq NM)   20.62   0.000   0.000%
D: 09/27/99   O: 10.25   H: 10.25   L: 8.88   C: 9.63   Y: 36.23

Prophet Financial Systems, Inc. (www.prophetfinance.com) Used by permission.

This chart illustrates two points about support and resistance. First, a group of people bought the stock in the $9 to $11 area and they are happy with a doubling of the price, so there is resistance in the $18 to $22 area. Second, dips in the $15 to $14 area represent the 50% retracement of the advance; other traders are buyers there in April and July.

retreats. Traders may not find the stock attractive as a buy again until it has retraced or pulled back one-third or even one-half of the amount gained in the rally. See Figure 5.7.

Percentage retracements, when measured from the high of a move, tend to act as a support area when the market retraces part of its rally. These same percentage levels, when measured from the low of a move down, tend to act as a resistance area.

The more popular and widely followed retracements include 25%, 33%, 38%, 50%, and 66% retracement points. These percentages correlate to the common fractions of $1/4$, $1/3$, $3/8$, $1/2$, and $2/3$. They are common places to look for support when prices correct within an uptrend. These percentage retracements can also be applied to find resistance areas when prices bounce in a downtrend.

Other retracement percentages are derived from the Elliott Wave approach or the application of the Fibonacci number series; but retracements are guidelines, and you should not make things too complicated when they don't have to be.

Price Objectives

Price objectives, from bar chart patterns and point-and-figure charts, can give you ideas on where to look for support and resistance. If a large ascending triangle in an uptrend gives you a price objective of $60 from the breakout point, it is logical to expect to see some profit taking, some hesitation, and some resistance in that area. An obvious head-and-shoulders bottom pattern may measure to $56. Traders who saw the pattern and acted on it are likely to take profits at the price target; then selling resistance will develop. See Figure 5.8.

Moving Averages

Moving averages are simply mathematical representations of the trend. Therefore, they can act as support and resistance just as trend lines can. You will often find the 50-day and 200-day moving averages will act as key support in a bull phase and as resistance in a bear phase. A simple moving average is shown in Figure 5.9.

Figure 5.8: A 1-Year Daily Bar Chart Showing a Triangle Pattern

Agnico Eagle Mines   10.84   0.000   0.000%
D: 01/16/01   O: 6.25   H: 6.31   L: 6.12   C: 6.19   Y: 12.04

Prophet Financial Systems, Inc. (www.prophetfinance.com) Used by permission.

A 3-month triangle pattern is $2 in height. This is projected upward from the breakout at $8.75 and gives a target of $10.75, which tends to act as a resistance area.

Figure 5.9: A 1-Year Daily Bar Chart with a 50-Day Simple Moving Average

At&t Corp   19.09   -0.019   -0.104%
D: 01/21/00   O: 52.13   H: 52.56   L: 51.00   C: 52.38   Y: 64.91

Simple Moving Avg.

Prophet Financial Systems, Inc. (www.prophetfinance.com) Used by permission.

Here the 50-day simple moving average acts like a smoothed trend line and resistance. Notice how the rallies in the downtrend fail at or near the moving average, giving you another tool to find resistance or support.

EXTRAPOLATING TREND LINES

Trend lines can be used to find support and resistance levels if you extrapolate them. Trend lines will find buying and selling at the imaginary line we discussed in Chapter 4. The more times the stock touches the uptrend or downtrend line, the more valid the trend becomes and the more likely it is that the trend line will act as support or resistance. See Figures 5.10 and 5.11.

PRICE MARKUPS

Using multiples of a key low is another way to anticipate resistance. Let's assume the low of a stock was $10. Some traders would be expected to take profits at $20, which would be a doubling of the low. People think about their price targets in terms of movements from their entry level. Doubling is especially ingrained in our thinking. We take notice of two-for-one sales promotions and we often use the expression "double or nothing." See Figure 5.12.

Figure 5.10: A 1-Year Bar Chart with a Channel Projected into the Future

Wal-mart Stores 56.10 0.300 0.538%
D: 01/16/01 O: 53.44 H: 54.81 L: 53.19 C: 54.69 Y: 59.08

Prophet Financial Systems, Inc. (www.prophetfinance.com) Used by permission.

If this upward sloping channel continues, we are provided with a possible resistance area at $60 if the stock rallies.

Figure 5.11: A 5-Year Weekly Bar Chart Showing a Downward Sloping Channel

Archer-daniels-midland 13.91 0.000 0.000%
D: 01/20/97 O: 20.48 H: 20.48 L: 18.69 C: 18.93 Y: 27.25

Prophet Financial Systems, Inc. (www.prophetfinance.com) Used by permission.

This downward-sloping channel lasting two years provides many places to expect support and resistance levels.

Figure 5.12: A Long-Term Monthly Log Chart Showing Resistance Points Projected from Key Lows

At&t Corp 18.99 -0.119 -0.627%
D: 01/01/68 O: 8.52 H: 9.20 L: 8.37 C: 8.60 Y: 89.94

Prophet Financial Systems, Inc. (www.prophetfinance.com) Used by permission.

Notice on the long-term picture of AT&T how people who bought the stock (split adjusted basis) at $8 provided resistance at $16. People who bought it at $12 were sellers at $24, and people who bought under $16 got to sell up at $32.

VOLUME AT PRICE

A number of on-line systems and some Web sites display a technical tool called volume at price. This tool shows the volume of shares or contracts that were traded at each price. The volume is often displayed as a histogram with the bars running horizontally across the graph. The idea behind following volume at price is that the more volume that occurs at a given price level or area, the more valid the area will be as support or resistance. See Figure 5.13.

Figure 5.13: Volume at Price for IBM

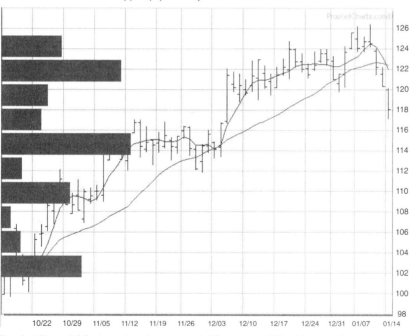

Prophet Financial Systems, Inc. (www.prophetfinance.com) Used by permission.

This chart shows a lot of volume at the $114 level, and this is also a level that acted as resistance on the rally up. The $114 level should act as support on the way down, and the amount of volume traded there supports that idea.

UNCHARTED TERRITORY

Before we leave the topic of support and resistance, I want to describe how to find support and resistance in virgin territory—an area where the stock has never traded before. To do this, you need to combine tools and learn from experience what works. Naturally we want to read the chart from right to left and look backward to see where we might expect support or resistance,

Figure 5.14: A Long-Term Monthly Log Chart Showing How to Project Support and Resistance

Johnson & Johnson 58.96 0.703 1.25%
D: 10/01/69 O: 0.969 H: 1.08 L: 0.958 C: 1.07 Y: 79.44

Prophet Financial Systems, Inc. (www.prophetfinance.com) Used by permission.

Johnson & Johnson has no overhead resistance, but this big channel tells us to expect resistance around $71, and that is also where the triangle formation during 2000–01 measures to. A point-and-figure count across the $50 area would also yield a price objective and next expected resistance.

but that is not always possible. We might be long in a stock that has broken out to a new all-time high. Great! But maybe we want to have an idea where we might encounter resistance or where to take profits. For resistance, we might use the return line of an uptrending channel (see Chapter 4). We could also use the upper band of a moving average envelope (see Chapter 11). We might use a doubling of the most recent resistance level; that should act as support on pullbacks. A big round number on the upside like $100, $150, or $200 might be considered as the next resistance. Of course, we can use a count from a point-and-figure chart for a longer-term target. Any and all of these techniques may work, along with a price target from a fundamental analyst. See Figure 5.14.

Patterns to Profit By

Now that you understand trend lines and support and resistance levels—the first two basic tools in technical analysis—you are ready to understand, look for, and project major top and bottom patterns. Just as you want to drill down with trends from the longest time frame to one you trade in so you gain important perspective, a similar concept holds when looking for chart patterns. You want to identify the major tops and bottoms first.

If you miss the major patterns, you will miss the big picture and probably the correct longer-term strategy. Short-term patterns repeat frequently and have limited price projections, but the major patterns let you know whether the sun is rising or setting, so to speak.

With all of these patterns it will be important to combine volume, the patterns' location with respect to the 52-week high and low, and some overall perspective, added to checking background news on the company and at the same time remaining flexible about the shape and complexity of the pattern. If you can spot the major top and bottom patterns, you will be way ahead of the game when looking at stocks to buy or avoid.

THE HEAD-AND-SHOULDERS PATTERN

One of the most common reversal patterns is the head-and-shoulders pattern. This is probably the best-known pattern by name among investors and traders. The head-and-shoulders may also be the most reliable pattern in terms of results, and has even been tested by the Federal Reserve. Unfortunately, its name does little to add credibility to the craft of technical analysis.

People who know little about technical analysis and its application often seize on the head-and-shoulders pattern as evidence of the lack of scientific support for technical analysis. How could serious investments be made on the basis of something that sounds a bit absurd? I suppose a pattern that was described by a serious-sounding list of numbers might be preferred, but this is the vocabulary we have inherited.

Another problem with head-and-shoulders patterns is that some novices will try to find them everywhere, recalling the expression that a little knowledge is a dangerous thing. Invalid head-and-shoulders patterns are often found in the wrong place or lack the correct volume pattern. Finally, this pattern may not have evolved over a long enough time period to be called a major top pattern.

HOW HEAD-AND-SHOULDERS PATTERNS ARE FORMED

The head-and-shoulders pattern in its simplest form is just three successive rallies and corrections or pullbacks, with the second rally reaching a higher point than the other two when we are looking at a top.

A head-and-shoulders top might form in a time span as short as three or four weeks, or it might evolve over a year or more. However, because it is a major pattern, it should take shape over two, three, or four months. When you stop to think about it, a period of around three months is logical when dealing with the stock of a publicly held company tied to the schedule of quarterly reports. As a quarter progresses and ideas about a company's fortunes shift, it is easier to expect a reversal in three months rather than in three weeks. A company might see some minor reversal in sales, for instance, for a few weeks, but an established company with a diversified product line and strong management can often make up a temporary dip by the end of the quarter. Also, as astute professional investors track a company, they may pick up subtle clues about sales, earnings, or competitors, and they begin to reduce their exposure to the company over the course of a quarter, rather than rapidly, over the span of just a few weeks.

Let's look at a generalized head-and-shoulders pattern and then look below the surface to understand what individuals and groups of investors may be doing. See Figure 6.1.

Figure 6.1: Generalized Head-and-Shoulders Top Pattern

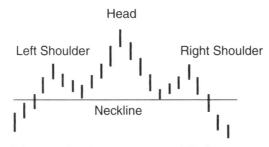

C. Recognia, Inc. (www.recognia.com) Used by permission.

This is the simple outline of what a head-and-shoulders pattern looks like, with a left shoulder, then a rally to a new high creating the head, followed by a third rally making a right shoulder. The distance from the neckline to the top of the head is measured and projected downward from the neckline to give an initial price target.

Now we need to find a stock that has been climbing and climbing for several months or even a couple of years, as the company and industry have been in favor. The head-and-shoulders top pattern is nothing more than a stock moving from an uptrend to a downtrend, and vice versa in the case of a head-and-shoulders bottom or an inverse head-and-shoulders pattern. See Figure 6.2.

Figure 6.2: A Long-Term Chart Showing the Major Rise Before the Head-and-Shoulders Top Pattern

Qwest Communications Intl Inc   7.56   0.070   0.935%
D: 06/23/97   O: 6.87   H: 7.53   L: 6.69   C: 7.14   Y: 71.16

Prophet Financial Systems, Inc. (www.prophetfinance.com) Used by permission.

A major top pattern like a head-and-shoulders must first have a big rise to reverse. From 1997 to the beginning of 2000, Quest had a rise from under $8 to over $60. This qualifies as a big rise that can be seen before a major top.

THE LEFT SHOULDER

The stock has rallied and reached a high on significantly higher volume. Prices react and pull back or correct, and the volume shrinks or dries up considerably. When compared to the volume on the next two rallies of the pattern, the left shoulder should have the heaviest volume. The stock holds at a support level (see Chapter 5) on the correction.

THE HEAD

The stock has another rally after the correction of the first rally. The stock carries up to a new high—higher than the first rally. Volume expands on the rally, but a peak in price is soon reached. Eventually, another reaction or downward correction develops on lighter volume, with the price declining back to a price level in the general vicinity of the first correction. We say general vicinity because it could be the same price level or higher or even slightly lower. The lows of the corrections can be joined now by a lateral trend line, which is called the neckline. (What else would you have expected to find below a head and two shoulders?) Typically, the neckline is upward-sloping or horizontal, as the corrections find support at nearly the same price level or higher.

THE RIGHT SHOULDER

The stock has a third rally that does not reach the same height as the head before its correction. Like the first two rallies, volume expands on the advance and decreases on the subsequent decline. If we look back at the three rallies, we should find that volume was the greatest on the first rally in the left shoulder, less on the head, and still less on the right shoulder. Volume should contract on the rally of the right shoulder and should be interpreted as a weakening of the price structure. This is because fewer and fewer people are optimistic about the price prospects for the company's stock, and investors have used the three rallies to reduce their exposure.

We now have the basic outline of a head and two shoulders, but the pattern cannot be considered complete until it breaks down below what has, for better or worse, been called the neckline. As mentioned earlier, the neckline is a line drawn connecting the lows of the left and right shoulders. Once the top pattern is complete and prices break down below the neckline, typically on heavy volume, they continue lower because the perception about the company has changed. Sometimes a stock breaks below the neckline and makes what is called a return move.

THE RETURN MOVE

The return move is basically a bounce that carries back up to the bottom of the neckline or the previous reaction low. The return move should stop at or short of the neckline, as holders of the stock who did not sell on the rallies or even when the neckline was broken are now motivated to try to break even or cut their losses with the stock bouncing back toward the neckline. The previous two lows or support levels now become resistance as they reverse roles.

The return move is typically on light volume and doesn't always occur. If the stock market as a whole is in a bull run and if the break of the neckline was not on heavy volume, the odds for a return move increase. But if the overall stock market is weak and a break of the neckline occurred on heavy volume, then the probability of a return move occurring is lower. This is shown in Figures 6.3 and 6.4.

It's important to understand who the buyers and sellers are and what they are doing as the head-and-shoulders pattern develops. The head-and-shoulders pattern actually begins long

Figure 6.3: A 2-Year Daily Bar Chart Showing Unorthodox Head-and-Shoulders Top Pattern

Prophet Financial Systems, Inc. (www.prophetfinance.com) Used by permission.

This unorthodox-looking head-and-shoulders top pattern in the spring and summer of 2000 on Intel Corporation shows the breakdown under the rising neckline, and the quick return move to the underside of the neckline, before the stock gaps down sharply on very heavy volume.

Figure 6.4: A 2-Year Daily Bar Chart Showing Complex Top Formation

Prophet Financial Systems, Inc. (www.prophetfinance.com) Used by permission.

Enron shows a huge distribution area (top) from $60 to $90 lasting approximately a year. The stock breaks the neckline around $68, dips, and then bounces before turning down sharply. If you saw this bearish top formation, you would expect something negative to happen.

before the three rallies appear, with an astute group of investors who buy the stock before the uptrend. These investors do their fundamental homework and position the stock in their portfolios when the stock is undervalued and probably not widely followed. These are the people who create the base on the stock. They may add to their positions during the major markup that eventually leads to the topping phase.

The early group of buyers does some selling into the left shoulder to less astute traders. Somewhere in the area of the left shoulder, the astute investors have decided that the market has discounted all the bullish news on the company, or their research may reveal that the fortunes of the company are shifting for the worse. The rally has a correction and pulls back to allow another group of investors to buy the "bargain" on the technical correction.

Volume on the rally of the left shoulder is strong; actually, it should turn out to be the strongest volume of the whole pattern. The market or stock rallies to a new high and other people who wanted to buy the dip but were slow or unconvinced now become convinced the stock is going higher when it makes new highs. So they reach and buy it, only to see another reaction when their buying is exhausted.

Of course, there are people who missed the advance and reaction and they now decide to buy the second pullback, as the last chance before it takes off again. The stock advances again, but volume is diminished and on this rally the people who bought on the head want to get out as best they can. The rally fails at a lower peak, with the early investors selling the rest of their holdings.

PRICE PROJECTIONS

One of the benefits of using bar charts and looking for the various price patterns is that these patterns, unlike candlesticks, give you price targets. To get a price projection from a head-and-shoulders top pattern, you measure the height—in points or dollars or euros or whatever unit you are operating in—from the neckline to the top of the head. This distance is then projected downward from the neckline, after the right shoulder.

For example, if the distance from the neckline to the top of the head is $14, then you subtract that from the intersection of the neckline at the point where the correction from the right shoulder touches the neckline. The result is your initial downside price objective. I use the word *initial* because the decline from a head-and-shoulders top formation can often carry farther than this target.

If the first target from the neckline is overrun, you can do a couple of things to get some guidance on where prices are headed. One approach is to double the initial price target; subtract another $14, or a total of $28, from the neckline. Another approach is to read the chart from right to left and find an area of resistance below the market that stalled the advance on its way to the top pattern. The farther back in time it occurred, the less reliable this level will be as a potential support level and valid price objective. Still another approach is to look for the one-half and two-thirds retracement points of the entire rally from the base to the top. This can also be combined with any big figure—a major price milestone like $100 or DJIA 10,000 or NASDAQ 1,000.

THE INVERSE HEAD-AND-SHOULDERS PATTERN

The head-and-shoulders bottom (or inverse head-and-shoulders pattern) looks like an upside-down head-and-shoulders top and marks the end of a downtrend instead of the end of an advance. See Figure 6.5.

Figure 6.5: A Generalized Head-and-Shoulder Bottom Pattern

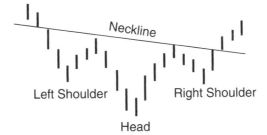

C. Recognia, Inc. (www.recognia.com) Used by permission.

This is the simple outline of a head-and-shoulders bottom pattern with a decline and rally to make a left shoulder, then another decline to a new low and rally creating the head, followed by a third decline and rally making a right shoulder.

THE LEFT SHOULDER

The stock or commodity or currency has been in a decline for some time. It has probably fallen out of favor with investors and is no longer on the most-active list. Prices finally reach a sort of climax on the downside and a normal trough in the trend appears. The market or stock rallies, but this advance peters out and another, lower trough or low is formed. Volume should expand on the decline but shrink on the rally.

THE HEAD

When the rally in the left shoulder ends and prices weaken, the decline carries to a new low, below the low point of the left shoulder. The volume or turnover increases on this second decline compared to the rally that preceded it, but it is less than the overall volume on the left shoulder.

THE RIGHT SHOULDER

A third decline develops but it does not reach the same low seen on the decline that formed the head. Another rally develops. Volume should decline markedly on this third decline and increase sharply on the next rally back up to the neckline, which connects the highs of the prior two rallies. Volume should remain high as the stock moves up through the neckline. A close watch should be kept on the volume on this rally from the right shoulder. If volume is not stronger than it was in the rest of the pattern, you should be particularly wary, even if the shape of the price pattern looks perfect. The increasing volume, as you progress through the pattern from left to right, tells you that more and more traders see the shifting improvement in the company's fortunes; but increasing volume from the right shoulder on up through the neckline is more important to show that a sustained bullish shift has occurred and the breakout above the neckline is likely to be sustained.

THE NECKLINE

As in the head-and-shoulders top pattern, a similar neckline can be drawn through the tops of the rallies from the left shoulder and head. The measurement technique is just reversed—you measure the distance from the bottom of the head to the intersection of the neckline. This distance in points or dollars is then added to the price of the neckline where it intersects with the rally of the right shoulder. A return move to the neckline may or may not develop; once again, that depends on whether the overall market is in a bull or bear phase.

Some traders believe that return moves are more likely to follow a bottom pattern than a top one, but I doubt if anyone has actually tested out this idea to see if it is valid. Return moves from breakouts of inverse head-and-shoulders patterns are profit-taking reactions. In the early stage of a new advance, a profit-taking correction seems intuitively more likely to occur, as some traders may not have confidence in the rally and are prone to take the quick profits.

DOUBLE TOPS AND BOTTOMS

These patterns are often compared to "M" or "W" patterns. Double tops and bottoms are probably the second most common major reversal patterns you will find when you examine charts. Also, they make a lot of sense when it comes to tactics and a shift in the market from bullish to bearish or from bearish to bullish.

Double Tops

A double top pattern looks like a large letter M, and some people actually call it an M formation. The double top pattern is a fairly reliable reversal pattern. Prices advance and have generally extended pretty far, then at some point fail to extend the advance and are followed by a breakdown to a new reaction low of about 5% or more from the first peak. Volume is usually heaviest on the first peak and builds again on the second rally attempt. Some investors or traders buy the reaction, betting that it is only a correction in an uptrend, but prices fail somewhere in the area of the first high. Prices turn down again and break down below the first reaction low—the double top has been made. Look for volume to expand when the market declines below the

Figure 6.6: A Generalized Double Top Pattern

C. Recognia, Inc. (www.recognia.com) Used by permission.

This simple diagram shows a classic double top pattern. A neckline can be drawn along the trough that separates the two peaks. The vertical distance between the neckline and the twin peaks is projected downward for an initial price target.

first reaction low. In some books on technical analysis, authors say that volume should be heavy around one or both peaks, or that any unusual change in volume, such as a decline in activity, will tend to confirm that you have identified a double top. See Figure 6.6.

DOUBLE BOTTOMS

The double bottom is just the reverse image of the double top, except for volume. Instead of an M, the double bottom pattern resembles the letter W. Prices decline to make an initial low and rally as shorts are covered and early bottom-pickers or bargain-hunters enter. The rally extends about 5% from the first low, but the rally doesn't hold and prices return to the prior low. The market finds support or buying interest around the prior low, and we have another bounce or rally from the twin bottom.

Unlike the double top, the volume increases on the rally from the second low. This is because more traders are encouraged, since the market held twice at the same level. Traders know to buy the pullback. If you buy the pullback, you know where you are wrong and what to risk. When you buy the pull-back, you have to risk only below the first low. If the market makes a new low, it is usually a good sign that further declines are likely. Also look for volume to increase when the high of the first bounce is exceeded. See Figure 6.7.

Figure 6.7: A Generalized Double Bottom Pattern

C. Recognia, Inc. (www.recognia.com) Used by permission.

Here we have the mirror image of the double top, giving us the double bottom (sometimes called the W pattern). A neckline can be drawn along the peak that separates the two bottoms. The vertical distance between the neckline and the two troughs is projected upward for an initial bullish price target.

BEHIND THE PRICE ACTION

How do tops and bottoms occur? After a significant rally, the stock, commodity, or bond reaches a price level at which there is enough supply put on the market to stop the rally and start a downward reaction. The security or market pulls back, at least 5% from the peak, until bargain-hunters or short-term traders who have been waiting for a dip to buy begin to buy the stock.

This is the first reaction low. From this low, the market ral-lies back to the first high, where sellers who did not take their profits on the first move up now decide to seize the opportunity and sell in the area of the first top. This selling creates the second peak of the double top.

Supply and profit-taking appear again, in addition to sales by earlier buyers, and prices decline down through the first reaction low. Volume is usually heavier at or near one or both peaks.

Price Targets

The double top pattern will also yield a price objective. The distance traveled between the first reaction low and the two tops of the double top is measured in points or dollars and projected downward from the reaction low to get a price target. If the price target is overrun with the market still falling, as with the head-and-shoulders pattern, a doubling of the first target can be used as an objective or target. Double tops and double bottoms may not be expected to top at exactly the prior high or low, but rather 1% or 2% above or below the first peak.

Remember how investors and traders tend to think to understand why I suggest looking for the second peak of the double top anywhere from 2% below the prior high to 2% above. Traders who bought or went long anywhere near the first peak are probably anxious to get out at break-even if they held on to the stock on the decline to the low. Rather than holding out for the last few fractions of the first high, these traders often begin selling before the high.

Other traders may be bearish and are going short as the stock gets up near the old high. The shorts, if they are smart, place a buy stop at or over the top of the first peak. If prices rally enough on the second peak, they can reach those protective buy stops and drive the market over the top of the first peak.

The action of the profit-taking and the stop-loss orders gives us that −2% to +2% band around the first high. If the stock stops lower than 2% below the first high, we might be watching an equilateral triangle, and if the stock exceeds the prior high by more than 2%, it is more likely that it will keep rising.

TRIPLE TOPS AND BOTTOMS

Another major top or bottom pattern is the triple top or triple bottom. This involves the same basic market action and volume characteristics as a double top or bottom, but a third peak or bottom will be formed.

The triple top is formed when there are three roughly equal peaks in an uptrend or advance, and is completed when the price breaks below the lows of the troughs. See Figures 6.8 and 6.9.

Figure 6.8: A Generalized Triple Top Pattern

C. Recognia, Inc. (www.recognia.com) Used by permission.

You know what a double top looks like, so for a triple top you look for one more rally that ultimately fails. A neckline can be drawn connecting the two lows that separate the rallies, and the distance from the neckline to any of the peaks can be used as a price target.

The triple bottom is formed when there are three roughly equal troughs after a downtrend. The triple bottom is completed when the price breaks out above the high of the peaks from the rallies off the bottoms. See Figures 6.10 and 6.11.

Volume should be examined, if available, to confirm these patterns. Volume should expand less during the forming of the second peak or trough than during the formation of the first peak or trough. Moving over to the third peak or trough, you should see volume expand less than on the second peak or trough. However, volume should expand on the breakout through the lows or highs of the peaks or troughs.

Figure 6.9: A 5-Year Weekly Bar Chart Showing Triple Top Formation

At&t Corp 19.11 0.210 1.11%
D: 01/13/97 **O:** 25.74 **H:** 26.07 **L:** 25.00 **C:** 25.25 **Y:** 62.32

Prophet Financial Systems, Inc. (www.prophetfinance.com) Used by permission.

A massive 15-month triple top formation can be seen on AT&T before it starts on the road down from $60 to $16. The old saying, "the bigger the top, the bigger the drop," can be applied to this chart example.

Figure 6.10: A Generalized Triple Bottom Formation

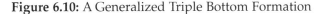
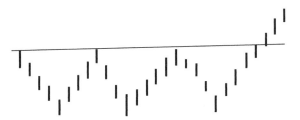

C. Recognia, Inc. (www.recognia.com) Used by permission.

The triple bottom is the mirror image of the triple top. Draw a neckline connecting the two peaks of the rallies, and the distance from the neckline to any of the lows can be used as a price target by adding to the breakout point.

Figure 6.11: A 1-Year Daily Bar Chart Showing Two Triple Bottoms

Computer Sciences   49.20   -0.779   -1.55%
D: 01/12/01   O: 55.38   H: 58.25   L: 55.19   C: 56.69   Y: 64.78

Prophet Financial Systems, Inc. (www.prophetfinance.com) Used by permission.

A smaller triple bottom can be seen during June and July on this stock, but notice the larger, irregular triple bottom from March through October.

Triple tops or triple bottoms use the same measuring technique to target a move down or up. The target for the triple top comes from measuring the distance or height of the pattern from the lowest low of the troughs to the highest point of the three peaks. The distance is projected downward from the point where the support is broken, from the breaking of the neckline. In a similar manner, the target from the triple bottom is taken from the bottom of the lowest point of the pattern to the highest high of the rallies in the pattern. This distance in points or dollars is projected upward once the resistance level is broken.

Naturally, we can't expect the three peaks in a triple top to line up exactly at the same high, so a triple top can be confused with a head-and-shoulders top pattern. Likewise, the bottoms of a triple bottom formation are not expected to hit all at the same price, so this pattern could be seen as an inverse head-and-shoulders pattern.

As a practical matter, the end result and the targets work out to be the same thing. If the triple top or triple bottom goes on to form additional peaks or troughs, the pattern should be considered a rectangle formation (which can be a continuation pattern). The target from a rectangle is derived the same way as from a triple top or bottom.

SPOTTING A MAJOR REVERSAL PATTERN

When trying to determine if you have found a major reversal pattern, it is helpful to keep in mind that all major top and bottom reversal patterns should have certain key ingredients. First and foremost, there should be something to reverse. Does it make sense to look for a head-and-shoulders top pattern when the stock has rallied from $20 to $28? Not really, but a move from $20 to $80 gives you something to reverse.

The next thing to look for is whether the stock or market has reached a key price objective. If a major price objective has been reached, it can mean that the stock could undergo distribution or accumulation—with investors getting out of old long positions or into new long positions. Is the pattern broad enough to suggest that something more than a dip or a brief rally is going to develop?

In addition to the price action, you should be alert for anything unusual in the way of price or volume activity. A buying or selling climax can be important to help separate continuation patterns from reversals.

Triple tops and bottoms could be considered variations of double tops and bottoms. Volume declines from the first peak to the second and the third in a top pattern, and volume builds as a bottom develops and more people become aware of a turn and want to participate on the upside. Another thing to be aware of is that fear is probably a stronger emotion than greed, so it may take only one failure to move higher to worry investors, but it may take two or more tests of a low before traders have enough confidence in a stock to buy it.

When looking for double or triple tops and bottoms, you should not look for a small pattern or one that has formed quickly. Ideally, you should find a big pattern that has taken months to develop. You want to see a decline or rally of about 5% from the first peak or low. Be aware of whether the broad market is in a downtrend or uptrend. Look at the chart history of the instrument. Does it have a tendency to form double tops or bottoms at major turning points? Is the bottom or top forming at a target or a long-range support or resistance level? Yes it's a lot to consider all at once, but nobody said it was easy. To get some experience, look at the bottoms made during October-November of 1998.

MORE PATTERNS TO LOOK FOR

Technicians have found other patterns over the years, but you may not encounter them very often.

BROADENING TOPS

A broadening top pattern is another reversal to be alert for. Volatility increases as the market swings back and forth on speculative excesses. The pattern looks like a backward symmetrical triangle or the bell of a musical instrument. Figure 6.12 shows a broadening top.

SAUCERS

Sometimes a saucer top or bottom develops. The saucer pattern looks like a flattened out U at a bottom. You might also see it as a kind of blurred triple bottom without much amplitude between the peaks and troughs. Saucers are more likely to be found in quiet markets. Volume tends to track the shape of the saucer, declining to the trough and then building up again. After the saucer has formed, you might find that prices move sideways and make a "platform" before breaking out on the upside decisively.

Figure 6.12: A 6-Month Daily Bar Chart with a Broadening Formation

Intl Business Machines 119.42 -0.889 -0.739%
D: 07/17/01 O: 106.10 H: 108.58 L: 104.75 C: 108.53 Y: 131.53

Prophet Financial Systems, Inc. (www.prophetfinance.com) Used by permission.

Here we have a 6-week broadening formation on IBM. This expanding triangle-shaped formation usually occurs at tops and is very hard to trade as the market swings back and forth until the breakout. The best approach is to wait for the breakdown and then put on a trade (short). A move above the last high tells you that you are wrong.

Saucer tops (or rounding tops, as they are sometimes known) look like triple tops without much amplitude. Prices roll over, with several failed attempts to move higher. The volume pattern usually builds into the top "tick" and then diminishes until the breakdown point. It is hard to establish a neckline and obvious breakdown point for a saucer top, but at some point volume should expand as people react to the formation and a downtrend begins in earnest. See Figure 6.13.

A saucer bottom formation is shown in Figure 6.14.

Figure 6.13: A 3-Year Weekly Bar Chart with a Saucer Top Formation

Prophet Financial Systems, Inc. (www.prophetfinance.com) Used by permission.

Use your imagination to see how the S&P 500 index rolls over in a saucer top formation from 1,300 in April 1999, up to 1,550 in early 2000, and rolls back to 1,300 in the first quarter of 2001. Other rallies and failures don't stand out like a head-and-shoulders or even a triple top formation. The end result is nevertheless bearish.

Figure 6.14: A 3-Year Weekly Bar Chart Showing a 2-Year Saucer Bottom Formation

Prophet Financial Systems, Inc. (www.prophetfinance.com) Used by permission.

Notice how prices on SVM have slowly bottomed out between $14 and $9, over the course of two years. This shallow saucer bottom should still support a decent rally, when it gets going.

LINE PATTERNS

Another set of patterns you might encounter is the line bottom formation or long base and the line top. These patterns are not exciting, formed by a long sideways movement on the chart within a narrow range. Volume is pretty much level through the pattern, which makes sense because the market is staying in a tight range. Eventually, prices break out on the upside from a long base or on the downside from a top. A return move back to the breakout point may or may not develop before a sustained uptrend develops, in the case of a long base. See Figure 6.15.

Other variations may be encountered, like double bottoms and double tops with platforms. These platforms are small consolidations before the main trend gets under way. (It has been

Figure 6.15: A 2-Year Line Chart with a 7-Month Line Bottom Formation

Prophet Financial Systems, Inc. (www.prophetfinance.com) Used by permission.

JDS Uniphase is in the process of making a long line formation around the $10 level. This pattern usually lacks volume, besides the dull price action. If the line pattern becomes a long base, it can support a big upside move.

Figure 6.16: A 2-Year Daily Bar Chart with a Double Bottom and a Platform

Parker Drilling   3.60   -0.119   -3.22%
D: 07/13/00   O: 5.87   H: 5.87   L: 5.75   C: 5.81   Y: 7.36

Prophet Financial Systems, Inc. (www.prophetfinance.com) Used by permission.

Parker Drilling can show some big percentage swings in a small time frame. A double bottom around $4.20 in December has an initial thrust up, but the stock makes a sideways platform for three weeks before the sustained rally. The platform allows more buyers to get on board.

noted that platforms occur more often on double bases than on double tops, but there is no explanation as to why that happens. Perhaps traders hesitate less at tops than at bottoms.) Figure 6.16 shows a double bottom with a platform.

THE CUP-AND-HANDLE PATTERN

The cup-and-handle pattern might be considered another formation, but I would call it a saucer pattern with a platform. Cup-and-handle patterns were popularized by William O'Neil of *Investor's Business Daily,* and some analysts and traders like working with that formation. See Figure 6.17.

Figure 6.17: A 1-Year Daily Bar Chart with a Cup-and-Handle Formation

Interpublic Grp Cos 28.12 0.090 0.321%
D: 01/17/01 O: 46.00 H: 47.31 L: 45.88 C: 47.19 Y: 45.97

Prophet Financial Systems, Inc. (www.prophetfinance.com) Used by permission.

The cup on ITG forms from $23 to $18 during September to November. The stock moves up on volume, but then the handle forms around $28 to $30, making the base ultimately bigger. Go long on a breakout above $31.

V TOPS AND BOTTOMS

V tops and V bottoms can also be considered major patterns; they are interesting and dangerous at the same time. In the other patterns we have covered, there is a more gradual shift from bullish to bearish or from bearish to bullish. With a V (or spike) top or V (or panic) bottom, the turn comes with little or no warning. A V pattern can be broken down into three components; let's examine what happens with a V bottom.

The downtrend marks the first part of the V pattern. The decline should be sharp and deep, but other variations can work. Prices decline until the low point or pivot of the decline. The second part is that a single day may mark the low in a climax or washout, or it may take a few days of price action such

Figure 6.18: A 1-Year Daily Bar Chart with a V Bottom Pattern

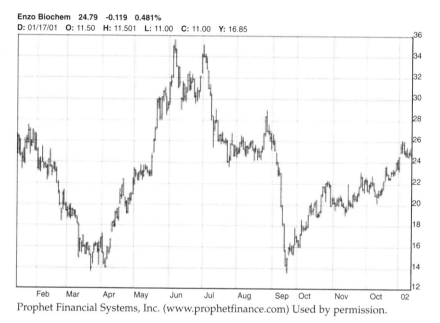

Enzo Biochem 24.79 -0.119 0.481%
D: 01/17/01 O: 11.50 H: 11.501 L: 11.00 C: 11.00 Y: 16.85

Prophet Financial Systems, Inc. (www.prophetfinance.com) Used by permission.

You can see a double top at $35 during June, but the sharp move down in September from $29 to under $14 is a classic V or spike bottom pattern. V bottoms (and tops) are very difficult to trade. Note how the old support in March held at $14.

as a 2-day reversal. Volume will be heavy on this turning point. In the third part, prices reverse to the upside. Volume tends to pick up on the move from the pivot low, and you probably break a downtrend line somewhere in the ensuing rally. There is also likely to be some symmetry in the price action in that, if prices decline at a 45-degree angle into the pattern, we are likely to see prices rally at the same angle out of the low. See Figure 6.18.

In the final analysis, it is not the name of the pattern or the shape that matters. What's important is whether you see a strong pattern or a weak pattern, whether the rallies are getting weaker with volume diminishing, whether the declines are failing to make new lows, and whether the volume is building toward a good base.

Reversals Can Keep You on Your Toes

When you look for price patterns, you generally look at days and weeks and months of price activity. You are looking for a slower transition as supply and demand battle for the upper hand. But when you look for 1-day, 2-day, or 2-week reversals, you need to be focused on the short-term day-to-day activity. Because these reversals can mark a major shift in the performance of the stock, commodity, or bond, you will need to be on guard for these patterns even if you are a self-professed long-term investor.

THE TOP REVERSAL DAY OR BUYING CLIMAX

Imagine that you find a stock that has been rising for several months, making a substantial advance, and sentiment about the stock or industry is bullish. It rallies to a new high for the move up, and then hits heavy selling. The stock drops back from being up on the day to the unchanged level, and then to down on the day. The stock may decline even further, and it closes well below the close of the prior day.

To put it another way, the stock goes from being up strongly at a new high to down on the day, giving everybody who bought it on the close of the previous day or higher and everyone who bought it on the reversal day an unpleasant loss. This description of a new high for the move up and a loss for the day is called a top reversal day, and can also be called a buying climax. Top reversal days may be only interruptions in an uptrend, but if a major shift to a downtrend occurs, then the pattern is called a key reversal day.

It will take several days to determine that a new downtrend has begun. My rule of thumb is, the bigger the high–low range of the day *and* the heavier the volume, the more likely that we have a key reversal. What is more difficult to determine is whether sentiment swings from bullish to bearish in the day; this might be because of an earnings report or some other news event. That evening or the next day, you might see a headline announcing that "XYZ Corporation closes lower despite better earnings," or somewhere in the article see a quote that "earnings couldn't be better."

The headline reflects the discounting mechanism of the marketplace (which we discussed in Chapter 2). The quote needs to be interpreted to understand it. If earnings or business couldn't be better, then what is the most likely course of the future? Things will get worse, right? Obviously, because they can't get any better.

Several other points should be kept in mind when trying to determine whether a top reversal should be given closer attention. We said that a good rise in prices should precede the reversal. During this rise, we should not see a correction, but only limited, shallow dips. A sustained rise without a correction means a lot of pent-up profit-taking can develop, just when a trigger occurs.

Another guidepost occurs when the chart shows that all measurable price objectives have been exceeded, and the instrument is overbought. This combination would make it more likely you will see a correction, whereby longs cut and run or new shorts seize the opportunity to capture a downside move.

Buying panics and key reversals may be easier to spot on major stock indexes or exchange-traded commodities because the market is in a sense more concentrated and followed by the business media. Unfortunately, smaller companies are not on the radar screens of the major news services and the popular Web sites. Research departments of brokerage houses and news services can't be knowledgeable about every security under the sun. The end result is that the large firms tend to get the attention. Sales or assets are usually used as the yardstick for coverage.

These companies are followed because they have millions and millions of shares outstanding and ownership extends to many thousands of individuals and mutual funds. These companies get the attention of the media because the viewership or readership wants to know about them. Not unlike sports or weather coverage, we want to know about what affects us directly.

Small companies often hire publicity or media firms to try to get their message out to potential investors. The investor relations department of a smaller company may be more responsive to your requests for information than the same department in a Fortune 500 corporation.

SPIKE DAYS

In some technical literature you will find the term *spike days*. A spike high day is a trading session whose high is sharply above the high of the preceding *and* subsequent or succeeding days. Most often, the closing price of the spike high will be near the lower end of the trading range for the day. A spike high day can occur without the substantial advance you want to see before a top reversal day or buying climax.

Like many other indicators, the importance of a spike high day increases if there is a big difference between the spike high and the highs of the days before and after the spike day. You also want to see a close near the low of the range for the day, *and* you want to see a good price rally leading up to the spike high. See Figure 7.1.

Some commodity traders use another variation of the key reversal day. They follow the same description of the key reversal day, but they look for a close below two prior days to give more validity to the pattern. This variation means that most of the longs put on over the preceding three days are likely to be at a loss at the close of the top or key reversal day. Imagine how many more people will want to get out of their losing long positions on the opening of the next session, when the buying action of three days of trading is at a loss.

With commodity traders using leverage and precious trading capital changing quickly, this signal is powerful and is usually not ignored. If on day four, the day after the signal, you close

Figure 7.1: A 3-Month Daily Bar Chart of Enzo Biochem Showing Upside and Downside Key Reversals

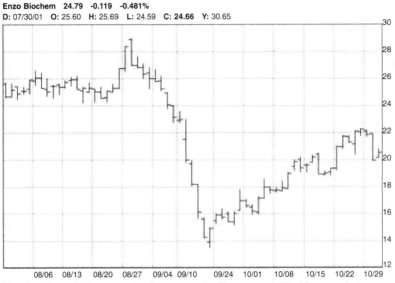

Enzo Biochem   24.79   -0.119   -0.481%
D: 07/30/01   O: 25.60   H: 25.69   L: 24.59   C: 24.66   Y: 30.65

Prophet Financial Systems, Inc. (www.prophetfinance.com) Used by permission.

You have to be nimble to trade this stock. At $29 at the end of August, we make a key reversal to the downside, and in the two weeks after the September 11 period we reverse to the upside, but not until the stock has quickly lost 50% of its value.

lower, you might have 80% (four out of five days) of a weekly reversal signal. A weekly reversal obviously has more meaning than a 1-day reversal. See Figure 7.2.

The 1-day key reversal day (spike day) is next on our list. The 1-day key reversal day might be misunderstood or fuzzy at this point. It is essentially a top reversal pattern in which prices eventually start a sustained downtrend. The true key reversal day is only known with some hindsight, when prices have already moved significantly lower.

2-DAY AND 2-WEEK REVERSALS

Sometimes a reversal takes two days to form. There doesn't seem to be a good explanation for why some stocks, indexes, or

Figure 7.2: A 3-Month Daily Bar Chart Showing Upside and
Downside Key Reversals

Textron Inc   41.25   -2.16   -4.99%
D: 10/12/01   O: 37.05   H: 37.05   L: 36.27   C: 36.86   Y: 45.45

Prophet Financial Systems, Inc. (www.prophetfinance.com) Used by permission.

Textron Inc. is another stock that turns on a dime. In late October we reverse to the upside from the $32 area. The next reversal happens in January, when we briefly push above $44. The stock holds for two days before breaking lower.

other securities can reverse in one day, and others need two days. It might be a function of the news or the kind of traders and investors in the company. It may be because some reversals don't occur until the next morning.

Traders may go home bullish on Tuesday, and depending on some overnight news or just the lack of expected follow-through buying for Wednesday morning, the sentiment shifts and traders want to be sellers. Traders who believed they bought a breakout to a new high now regret that they may have paid too much. The market closes weak on the second day, near the lows.

This combination of a high close followed by a low close is called a 2-day reversal. Trading volume should be high on the two days in question. Like a top reversal, the 2-day reversal is not necessarily a major reversal. Given the right combination of factors or circumstances, the 2-day reversal is worth following closely. Again, the odds improve if prices traverse a big range; there is high volume and a reversal in sentiment.

A 2-week reversal can be spotted easily on weekly charts, and will appear to be more rapid and powerful at a top than at a bottom. This is probably because more people are involved in the stock after an advance than after a decline.

OUTSIDE DAYS

Outside days come in two varieties—with higher or lower closes. An outside day is a session or day in which the high–low range of the current day is outside or eclipses the prior day. In other words, today's high is higher and today's low is lower than yesterday's high and low. This is shown in Figure 7.3.

Outside days may occur in a sideways or trendless period when prices are consolidating, but these examples don't carry the same meaning or potential. When an outside day develops in a trend, it can be a sign of weakness or it can mark a reversal.

Outside days occur when one side of the market—bulls or bears—has been in control for part of the day, but the opposite side is able to gain control for part of the day. There is uncertainty as to who is in control, and as a result, the market is prone to a change of control. An outside day in a trend can also be interpreted as a sign of weakness, foreshadowing a reversal.

Consider what goes on during an outside day in an uptrend or downtrend. For part of the session, the side of the market that has been in control continues to be in control. But for part of the session, the other group takes control so that the high or low is broken. The stock has probably seen a widely swinging day and the direction seems a little uncertain. What is certain is that the group that was in control has lost some of its commitment, and therefore the stock is susceptible to a change in control.

The outside day can mean the stock is going to take a short rest after a strong move up or down, but it can also mean that a new trend in the opposite direction could begin. Outside days often develop after a strong move up or down, on a wide-

Figure 7.3: An Outside Day Pattern

In its simplest form, an outside day has a higher high and a lower low than the prior day (or week). It is called an outside day because the range of the bar is completely outside the range of the previous bar.

Created by the author.

ranging day. This wide-ranging outside day can be followed by a trading range type of market, as prices correct what was probably an overbought or oversold condition. But when the open and the close or even the close alone are in the opposite direction of the previous trend, we can see a reversal.

Let's look at an outside day and a lower close after a rally. Prices have been trending higher in a nice uptrend. The trend is strong, volume has expanded, and there are good profits built up by the longs. Let's imagine on the day of the outside day that prices open lower, down from the previous day's close. Buyers come in to snap up shares or contracts to take advantage of what they believe is a temporary bargain before the uptrend resumes. Prices firm to the unchanged level and then go up on the day as more buyers enter, encouraged by the ability of the stock to rebound from a lower open.

Buyers push the market up and up, even exceeding the highest price paid during yesterday's trading. Everyone who bought this morning is happy, but the rally doesn't hold. There is profit-taking by people who are long, did not get out yesterday, and have been biting their nails ever since the lower opening.

Other selling comes from people who sense that prices are too high or the item is too expensive. Prices slip lower and lower, and we close down on the day. We don't really know that the bears have now gained control of the market, but we have seen a lot of profit-taking and other selling.

An outside day and lower close can also start out with prices opening higher and then failing after the prior day's high is exceeded. The bulls are caught long and then the market slips lower, unable to hold above yesterday's high. Traders liquidate early longs as the market's performance disappoints. Prices move lower until we reach the unchanged level. Once any support at this level is broken, we find more people willing to sell when prices have slipped into the minus column. Bulls are caught and are left disappointed by the close, but with a lower open we find even more people are disappointed by the close.

Futures traders often seize on outside days with lower closes as short-term top reversals, and put protective buy stop orders over the high of the outside day. Similarly, they can mark key lows with an outside day and a higher close after a decline. The success of an outside day and a higher close marking a low is enhanced if we are near a major support area. See Figure 7.4.

Figure 7.4: A 6-Month Daily Bar Chart with an Outside Day and Lower Close

Amgen Inc-(Nasdaq NM) 55.50 -1.59 -2.79%
D: 01/22/01 O: 70.00 H: 70.87 L: 66.31 C: 67.62 Y: 70.17

Prophet Financial Systems, Inc. (www.prophetfinance.com) Used by permission.

The arrow points to an outside day with a lower close at the end of February. The reversal occurs at the prior resistance of $75 that stopped the advance during the middle of February. The stock trades sideways for the few days before the move down starts in earnest.

INSIDE DAYS

I am including inside days in this chapter even though they are not exactly reversals. An inside day is one in which the range of the current day is entirely within the high–low range of the prior day. This means that the high is lower than the previous high and the low is higher than previous low. When inside days are seen occurring in a trend, it can be viewed as a sign of weakness and may precede the start of a reversal. When you see a market in an uptrend or a downtrend, you know that the bulls or bears are in control. When an inside day occurs, it shows that neither camp is able to move the market or stock to new ground on the upside or downside.

The inside day also means that neither the longs nor the shorts are able to gain the upper hand, but the group that was in control has lost some commitment; thus, the market is now prone to a change. That is why inside days are potentially a sign of weakness. An inside day after a strong move can also mean that the market is pausing or catching its breath, so to speak, after the strong move. See Figure 7.5.

Figure 7.5: A Simple Inside Day Pattern

Reduced to its simplest form, an inside day has a lower high and a higher low than the previous bar. The range of the bar is completely within the range of the prior bar. An inside day tells you that neither the bull nor the bear was successful, but the next move up or down could decide the market's direction, and thus it can become a reversal.

Created by the author.

EXCEPTIONS ARE THE RULE

As with other aspects of technical analysis, you will find examples that are not clear-cut. There are always exceptions and borderline cases. You might find yourself looking at a situation whereby the high or the low of the current day is equal to the prior high or low, rather than inside it or outside it. This is one of those gray areas where you could include these patterns or ignore them. You can argue it either way. Don't get stuck on precise rules; examine each situation and be alert for trend reversals. These borderline situations may result in more sideways trends, because while they may not develop into reversals, they do show the trend is losing strength or integrity.

A CLOSE ABOVE THE HIGH OF THE LOW DAY

This situation can also be described as a pivot point reversal. I learned about this indicator in the mid-1980s on the hedging and risk management desk of a regional dealer in fixed-income securities. The signal is really quite elegant when you get the knack of identifying the pattern. The stock has been in a downtrend and it makes a new low. If another new low is not made the next day *and* the stock can close above the high set on the recent low day, then we have a short-term buy signal, or at least a signal to cover shorts. The day the close is above the high does not have to be the second day. It could be day three, or four, or five, just as long as

Figure 7.6: A 6-Month Daily Bar Chart of Timken with a Close Above the High of the Low Day

Timken Co   16.24   -0.359   -2.16%
D: 07/16/01   O: 16.85   H: 17.10   L: 16.64   C: 16.70   Y: 17.16

Prophet Financial Systems, Inc. (www.prophetfinance.com) Used by permission.

The arrows show two examples of a close above the high of the low day. In September, the buy signal doesn't come till day three, but in early November, the reversal happens the next day. The pattern is fast and simple.

the stock does not make a new low. If it makes a new low, you have to start the process over again. This is very close in concept to a 2-day reversal signal, but the low day and the high close do not have to be together. The important thing to remember is that the stock has not made a new low, and all the shorts put on during the low day are at a disadvantage. See Figure 7.6.

A CLOSE BELOW THE LOW OF THE HIGH DAY

This is just the reverse of the pattern seen on the downside. The stock has had a rally and makes a new high. On day two, or three, or four, the market closes lower without making a new high for the price paid. The lower close must be below the low of the day when the stock made the high. Like a 2-day reversal signal, this could become a major sell signal if the stock continues to decline. See Figure 7.7.

Figure 7.7: A 9-Month Daily Bar Chart of Amgen with a Close Below the Low of the High Day

Amgen Inc-(Nasdaq NM) 55.50 -1.59 -2.79%
D: 04/16/01 O: 54.21 H: 56.00 L: 53.90 C: 54.58 Y: 69.95

Prophet Financial Systems, Inc. (www.prophetfinance.com) Used by permission.

This simple pattern of a closing below the low of the high day (which we know only with hindsight) gives you quick-turning top signals.

THE ISLAND REVERSAL

Another reversal worth learning about is the island reversal. Island reversals can be 1-day reversals, or they can include a small group of days or a cluster of days. In an uptrend, an island develops with a gap (see Chapter 9) or a price void from the high of the previous day to the low of the island day. The very next day, the market gaps down from the low of the island day to the high of the next day. See Figure 7.8.

Figure 7.8: A 6-Month Daily Bar Chart with a 2-Day Island Reversal

Intel Corp-(Nasdaq NM) 34.84 0.290 0.839%
D: 07/16/01 O: 30.03 H: 30.75 L: 28.77 C: 29.13 Y: 34.55

Prophet Financial Systems, Inc. (www.prophetfinance.com) Used by permission.

In early August, Intel gaps up to a new high, holds for one day, and then gaps lower, leaving the two days as an island separated by two gaps or price voids. The level later acts as resistance until we close above $32 in late November.

In a downtrend, the image is reversed. We have a gap down from the low of day one to the high of day two, the island. The next day, we gap up from the high of the island day to the low of day three.

The island reversal is more important the larger the gaps are on the chart. Examine the relationship between the open and close reversals in the first two sessions. In an uptrend, the close on day one is strong before the gap, and on the second day the market opens on its high and closes weak, but still leaves a gap. This points to a lower opening on day three. Also, an open on day two near the low of the day, followed by a close near the low, is also an indication of weakness on day three. The market gapped higher, pushed up during the day, but failed to hold most of those gains. This tells you the market was hitting resistance on a short-term basis.

An island reversal can also appear with a cluster of a few days—three, four, or maybe five—with prices holding above the gap created between day one and day two. Prices during this cluster of days hold in a relatively tight range before gapping down, leaving a small island pattern in their wake. See Figure 7.9.

Figure 7.9: A 6-Month Daily Bar Chart Showing a Bottom Island Reversal Day

Ryder System 23.51 -0.059 -0.254%
D: 07/16/01 O: 18.87 H: 18.98 L: 18.78 C: 18.92 Y: 23.56

Prophet Financial Systems, Inc. (www.prophetfinance.com) Used by permission.

Ryder makes a gap down and then gaps up the next day, creating a 1-day island bottom at $18 during the September plunge.

The island cluster reversal can also be seen at the end of a downtrend. In a downtrend, the gap down to the island is like a capitulation by longs that have held on and on, waiting for some kind of reversal. They finally give up hope and sell, giving us the gap lower. The gap down could come on news that is initially determined to be quite bearish. After the few days of sideways trading, the gap on the upside comes from a realization that the worst is over, and that the last move down was probably overdone. Island reversals that are seen on the upside seem to be created by shorts finally covering in a last gasp, or by some group of traders giving up on waiting for a reaction to buy, and finally jumping in on some bullish news, not wanting to miss any more of the action.

THE HOOK REVERSAL

The hook reversal is actually a specific kind of inside day. In an uptrend, a hook reversal starts with a session that has a lower high and a higher low than the prior day. In addition to that

Figure 7.10: A Hook Reversal after a Rally

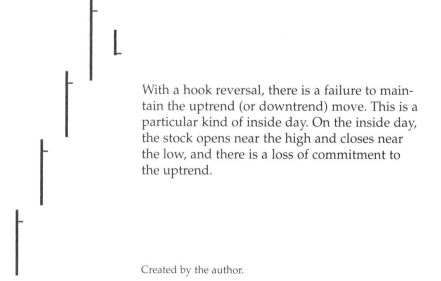

With a hook reversal, there is a failure to maintain the uptrend (or downtrend) move. This is a particular kind of inside day. On the inside day, the stock opens near the high and closes near the low, and there is a loss of commitment to the uptrend.

Created by the author.

inside day, you need to see the market open near its high and close near its low. In a downtrend, we start with an inside day in which you open near the low and close near the high. This is not a clear break in the trend, but a failure to maintain the trending move, up or down. This is a loss of commitment to the trend and can be the beginning of a reversal. See Figure 7.10.

Consolidations Are Great
Entry Points

Call them consolidation patterns or call them continuation patterns. These terms are pretty much interchangeable. In Dow Theory terminology, a sideways consolidation is known as a "line." Unlike the broad tops and bottoms taking two to three months or longer, most consolidation patterns occur in a few days or several weeks. If you don't have a position in a stock and you want to get aboard for the move up or down, you can use consolidations and retracements as entry points to get in.

FLAGS AND PENNANTS

Flags and pennants are two of the shortest or quickest formations of the various continuation patterns we'll discuss. These patterns most often occur early in an uptrend or downtrend. After a market has had a sharp move up or down, a period of consolidation may occur. This period of consolidation sometimes creates a formation called a flag or a pennant.

Watching the volume during these formations is key. In a bull market, the volume should be larger on the up days and smaller on the down days. During a bear market, the volume should be larger on the down days and smaller on the days when the market closes up. Both patterns develop quickly in strong trends and usually cover only a small price range.

BULL AND BEAR FLAGS

Bull flags start with a flagpole that is a sharp 1- or 2-day run-up on good volume, although some books describe the pole as the

125

strong trend before the reaction. In an uptrend, the rally attracts the attention of potential sellers. People see the run-up and want to take profits if they are long on the stock, commodity, or bond. The flag must be pictured without much of a breeze and will be a kind of parallelogram that is slanting downward by about 45 degrees. Prices drift irregularly downward as the potential sellers take their profits.

New buyers may appear on the dips to begin building a long position on weakness or to increase an existing position because they are now more bullish on the security after the high-volume pole. After this slightly sagging pattern has dipped and corrected enough, or some other piece of news comes along to inspire buyers, the market breaks out again in the direction of the prior trend, continuing the uptrend that was in force before

Figure 8.1: A Daily Bar Chart Showing Two Bull Flag Patterns

Deibold Inc 40.11 -0.929 -2.26%
D: 10/15/01 O: 39.63 H: 39.63 L: 38.68 C: 39.00 Y: 43.27

Prophet Financial Systems, Inc. (www.prophetfinance.com) Used by permission.

This chart shows two examples of a bull flag pattern in early November and late December. Note that volume is higher on the pole into the pattern, diminishes during the pattern as prices droop lower in a correction, and then expands once again as prices move higher from the body of the flag.

the pattern developed. The pattern is completed when the price breaks above the line drawn through the highs of the pattern. Two examples are shown in Figure 8.1.

Volume is important in identifying and trading flags and pennants. Volume should expand into the pattern, then contract or diminish overall as the pattern forms, and finally expand again as prices break out of the pattern. The price target from the flag pattern is simple, as the length of the advance into the pattern is added to the pattern on the breakout.

Bear flags are just the opposite pattern in a downtrend. Prices drop sharply for one or two days on good volume to form the pole, and then you should see the market drift upward at about a 45-degree angle for several days. Prices back and fill in a relatively tight range as volume contracts. This upward drift to prices gives short sellers a chance to add to positions, or others a chance to try to scalp the market. See Figure 8.2.

Figure 8.2: A Daily Bar Chart with a Bear Flag and a Pennant Formation

Prophet Financial Systems, Inc. (www.prophetfinance.com) Used by permission.

The February–March downtrend shows a bear flag pattern, and we have a nice example of a bullish pennant formation in the latter half of May.

BULL AND BEAR PENNANT FORMATIONS

The bull pennant is formed in the same way as the bull flag pattern illustrated in Figure 8.2, but instead of sagging in the breeze, the pennant makes its correction in a sideways or horizontal line, with prices coming more to an apex or point. The bull pennant begins with a sharp 1- or 2-day rally on good volume as some news event spikes prices to the upside. This is the pole to the formation. Volume diminishes as the pattern evolves but with the volume heavier on the up days and lighter on the down days. Volume is heavier on the rally up to the correction and diminishes through the pennant formation. Volume expands again as prices exceed the high of the pattern. See Figure 8.3.

Figure 8.3: A Daily Bar Chart with Pennant Patterns

Grainger (w.w.)   48.97   0.000   0.000%
D: 01/16/01   O: 35.94   H: 36.56   L: 35.63   C: 36.50   Y: 51.45

Prophet Financial Systems, Inc. (www.prophetfinance.com) Used by permission.

Pennants and flags can appear often; this chart shows three pennants as the stock rallies from $30 to $50. Notice how volume diminishes as each one develops.

The bear pennant will be found during declines in down-trends, in top formations, or in secondary reactions in bull phases. Bear pennants seem to take less time to form than bullish pennants, and this may relate to the nature of bear markets. Bear markets generally are shorter in duration than bull markets. The usual time relationship in a typical 4-year bull market in equities is a rally of three to three and one-half years, followed by a decline of one to one and one-half years. The tearing-down phase or bear phase is shorter because it takes a longer time to build up public participation in the rally, but on the downswing investors seem to flee in an instant. No one is interested in buying the dip, buyers back away, and bears come out of hibernation. A bear pennant may therefore last for only three or four days and not look like much of a pattern at all. See Figure 8.4.

Figure 8.4: A Daily Bar Chart with a Bear Pennant Formation

Deere & Co 43.00 -0.479 -1.09%
D: 02/15/01 O: 41.96 H: 42.50 L: 41.60 C: 42.05 Y: 46.07

Prophet Financial Systems, Inc. (www.prophetfinance.com) Used by permission.

Deere drops sharply from $41 to $38 and forms a bear pennant during May. From the breakout point, Deere drops approximately the $3 of the "pole" downward to nearly reach the $36 objective.

TRADING STRATEGY

The same trading strategy is used for both flags and pennants. In an uptrend, go long on a break above the line across the highs of the pennant or flag. A sell stop is placed below the lower boundary of the pattern, to exit if the expected rally reverses. In a downtrend, go short on a break below the line across the lows of the pennant, with a buy stop above the upper boundary of the pattern. Directions and trading strategies are easy to reverse for downtrends. See Figure 8.5.

Figure 8.5: A Daily Bar Chart with a Bear Flag Pattern and Stop-Loss Point

Helmerich & Payne   28.50   0.000   0.000%
D: 01/17/01   O: 42.81   H: 42.81   L: 40.75   C: 41.06   Y: 53.51

Prophet Financial Systems, Inc. (www.prophetfinance.com) Used by permission.

HP drops from $51 to under $45 to make the pole of this bear flag in May. The best strategy is to go short when the stock breaks under the lower trend line defining the flag, and then to risk or set a buy stop above the parallel upper trend line. In this example, if the stock trades back up to $48, the pattern is not working and a rally is under way.

TRIANGLES

There are three types of triangles: symmetrical, ascending, and descending. Triangles are primarily continuation patterns. There have been times when a large symmetrical triangle was a reversal pattern, but this is rare. Triangles should contain at least two distinct rallies and two distinct dips that serve as points of contact to draw the converging trend lines marking the triangle pattern.

THE SYMMETRICAL TRIANGLE

A symmetrical triangle can be thought of as a large pennant. (In some technical books, symmetrical triangles are known as coils.) The symmetrical triangle is formed in a trading range with lower highs and higher lows. It can occur in uptrends as well as downtrends, and indicates a balance in the supply–demand equation. Symmetrical triangles usually take several weeks to form and can be viewed as continuation patterns or sometimes as reversal signals when the price finally breaks out of the pattern, preferably on increased volume. Volume typically decreases or contracts through the formation of the pattern.

While I have not seen any supporting evidence, traders have suggested that a closer examination of the volume pattern within the symmetrical triangle can give you a better idea of the likely direction of the breakout. They suggest that you watch whether volume expands on the up- or downswings within the triangle, particularly the later swings, closer to the apex.

There is an old Wall Street saying that "volume precedes price." If the volume increases closer to the apex, it would probably mean that traders are getting more committed to one side of the market or the other and are stepping up their purchases or sales.

Because a trend in force tends to remain in force, the odds are that a triangle will eventually result in a continuation of the trend that preceded it. Of course, as with most things in life, there are no guarantees.

GET A SECOND OPINION

Using point-and-figure charts can be another way of trying to gauge the direction of the breakout from a symmetrical triangle. If you examine the price area where the triangle is forming with a relatively sensitive point-and-figure chart, you can see if there have been more tests of the upside or the downside. Assuming that markets trade in the direction of least resistance, the symmetrical triangle should break out in the direction with fewer tests. See Figure 8.6.

Figure 8.6: A Daily Bar Chart Showing a Symmetrical Triangle Formation

Prophet Financial Systems, Inc. (www.prophetfinance.com) Used by permission.

Notice how the stock moves sideways between contracting trend lines with volume contracting until the stock breaks out to the downside. The target of $24 comes from measuring the height of the triangle and projecting it downward from the breakout.

THE TARGET

How far will the market travel when it breaks out from the symmetrical triangle? Actually, the measurement technique is the

Figure 8.7: A Daily Bar Chart with a Symmetrical Triangle and Price Target

Gillette Co   32.14   0.000   0.000%
D: 01/16/01   O: 33.19   H: 34.38   L: 33.19   C: 34.13   Y: 33.65

Prophet Financial Systems, Inc. (www.prophetfinance.com) Used by permission.

Gillette makes a 4-week symmetrical triangle pattern in a downtrend. The height of the pattern is $3 and when the stock breaks out on the downside (the direction of the prior trend), the move carries $3 down, and more. Also notice how the ultimate low in the stock occurs where the triangle would have reached its apex (where the two trend lines converge).

same for all three types of triangles. The price range at the base of the triangle, where the first countertrend move occurs, is projected from the breakout point in the direction of the breakout. See Figure 8.7.

For symmetrical triangles, there is a shorthand method of measuring the price objective. Starting with the two trend lines you draw to frame the outline of the triangle, you can draw a line parallel to the side of the triangle that is opposite to the breakout. The breakout from the triangle is expected to carry to where that parallel line intersects. A simple example, shown in Figure 8.8, will make the technique clearer.

Figure 8.8: A Daily Bar Chart with a Symmetrical Triangle and Shorthand Price Target

Gillette Co   32.14   0.000   0.000%
D: 01/17/01   O: 34.19   H: 34.50   L: 33.56   C: 34.00   Y: 23.45

Prophet Financial Systems, Inc. (www.prophetfinance.com) Used by permission.

Here is the chart of Gillette from Figure 8.7, but without volume. A shorthand method of getting a price target is to draw a line parallel to the side of the triangle opposite to the breakout. The move up or down from the triangle usually ends on an extension of the parallel line; here it is overshot by a couple of dollars.

TIMING

Before we describe the ascending and descending triangles, a note is in order about a timing issue that seems to be unique to all triangles. I remember learning (in my very first course on technical analysis) that triangles rarely extend all the way out to the apex—that point where the pattern would have narrowed where the trend lines defining the triangle cross. Triangles typically break out two-thirds to three-quarters of the way through the pattern.

If you measure the triangle from the extreme left-hand side when the pattern begins, and extend the trend lines to an apex, you can quickly find the two-thirds point and the three-

quarters point of the pattern. With that knowledge, you are prepared for the breakout. You can also check the appropriate data
release calendar to see if there is a report due from the company
during that time window that could produce the breakout. See
Figure 8.9.

Here is another timing tool with triangles that I learned
from a bond trader. I am at a loss to explain why it might work,
but despite the lack of a logical explanation, I find it works well
in practice. This is how it is done: If you mark the point in time
where the triangle pattern would have reached its apex, that will
often mark the peak or trough of the move out of the triangle.
Examples in Figures 8.10 and 8.11 will show what I mean.

Figure 8.9: A Daily Bar Chart with Ascending Triangle and Timing of
Breakout

Prophet Financial Systems, Inc. (www.prophetfinance.com) Used by permission.

Ferro Corp. is in an uptrend when the ascending or bullish triangle
forms. Ferro breaks out over the supply line at $23.50, roughly two-
thirds of the way through the pattern if it went all the way out to the
apex where the two trend lines meet.

Figure 8.10: A Daily Bar Chart Showing Timing from the Triangle

Agnico Eagle Mines   10.70   -0.139   -1.28%
D: 01/16/01   O: 6.25   H: 6.31   L: 6.12   C: 6.19   Y: 12.28

This chart demonstrates two timing considerations from triangles. First, the triangle breaks out about three-quarters of the way through the pattern. Second, notice how a high is reached at approximately where the apex intersects.

Figure 8.11: A Daily Bar Chart Showing Timing from the Triangle

Engelhard Corp   26.27   -0.719   -2.66%
D: 01/16/01   O: 19.94   H: 20.91   L: 19.69   C: 20.75   Y: 29.45

Depending on how you draw the lower trend line of this triangle pattern, you will quickly see that the price low was reached at approximately that point in time where the apex would have occurred in September.

ASCENDING TRIANGLES

Ascending triangles have been called bullish triangles, rising triangles, and right-angle triangles, and they are the triangles you usually find in an uptrend. In the symmetrical triangle, we found that the two trend lines that formed the triangle came together at a 45-degree angle. With ascending triangles, the top line is as horizontal or as close to level as the supply line. This marks the price point where people are willing to offer stock and the advance is stopped.

Let's imagine that the stock rallied to the $50 level and found resistance. Sellers offer the stock and there is profit-taking. Buyers retreat or realize they don't have to bid aggressively for the stock when there is a ready supply at $50. The stock declines till bargain-hunters come in and the stock finds support. What follows is a series of rallies to the $50 supply line or area and subsequent corrections. As the buyers accumulate stock and the supply is reduced, the corrections don't go as deep. The buyers must raise their bids to get the stock they want as the supply is reduced.

What develops on the chart is an ascending demand line. The triangle forms from left to right as the horizontal supply line and the rising demand line converge. At some point, usually before the apex, demand overcomes the supply at $50 and the stock breaks out to the upside. While volume is usually lower during the triangle as the trading range shrinks, volume expands on the breakout.

Apply the same measuring technique we discussed for the symmetrical triangle to the ascending triangle. However, in a bull market, don't be surprised if the target is overshot. See Figure 8.12.

DESCENDING TRIANGLES

Descending, falling, or bearish triangles are found in downtrends and are upside-down versions of ascending triangles. In this pattern the stock declines until it reaches a level of support. Let's say the stock is coming down from $90 and buying develops at the one-third retracement level of $60. Buyers who missed the chance to buy the stock earlier come in to support the stock.

Figure 8.12: A Daily Bar Chart and Volume with an Ascending Triangle

Prophet Financial Systems, Inc. (www.prophetfinance.com) Used by permission.

Lockheed found resistance at $40 for about six months, until the rising support line absorbed all the supply and the stock broke out higher on heavy volume.

The stock rallies, some short sellers from $80 or $70 may cover, and the stock bounces till selling develops perhaps at $72. The bounce stalls and then the stock slips lower on renewed selling and maybe some liquidation from some of the new buyers at $60.

The stock declines to the $60 level again, and once again buying emerges, support develops, and the stock manages a rally back to $70 before resistance is encountered. The stock turns lower again and we have two points to connect—from $72 to $70—to form the resistance line or supply line of the triangle. Prices trade back and forth between the demand line at $60 and the descending supply line until the supply overwhelms the support at $60 and prices move lower.

Volume tends to diminish through the pattern as it contracts and then expands on the breakdown through the support, as traders who bought the stock at $60 turn into sellers and liquidate those trades along with others who may be long and don't want to see all their profits disappear. See Figure 8.13.

Figure 8.13: A Daily Bar Chart with a Descending Triangle

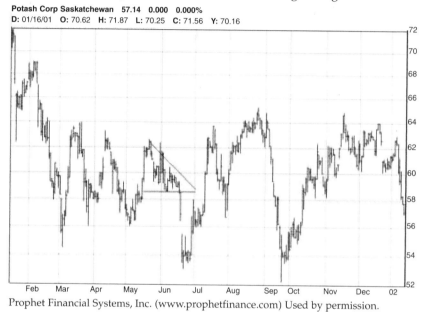

Potash Corp Saskatchewan 57.14 0.000 0.000%
D: 01/16/01 O: 70.62 H: 71.87 L: 70.25 C: 71.56 Y: 70.16

Prophet Financial Systems, Inc. (www.prophetfinance.com) Used by permission.

While the immediate trend into the triangle is not down, the trend in the prior three months is down. Here the stock quickly reaches the downside target of about $54.75 (the $58.25 support line minus the $3.50 measured from the height of the pattern).

TRADING STRATEGY

While the odds favor a breakout in the direction of the prior trend, that doesn't mean you have to go long or short anywhere within the triangle formation. Why tie up your money before the breakout when we know that some triangles can be reversal patterns? If you feel compelled to take a position before the breakout, then purchases should be made at the lowest possible levels within the triangle, or short sales made at the highest possible levels. Analysts generally consider the ascending triangle the most reliable for continuing the prior trend, followed by the symmetrical triangle, and then the descending triangle.

If you don't jump the gun, the trading strategy for triangles becomes trading in the direction of the breakout as soon as it happens, with a buy or sell stop at the other side of the triangle. If the triangle becomes a reversal pattern, close out the trade in the direction of the prior trend and enter a new position in the direction of the breakout with a stop-loss order on the other side of the triangle. See Figure 8.14.

Figure 8.14: A Daily Bar Chart with Trading Strategy

Molex Inc-(Nasdaq NM) 32.58 0.000 0.000%
D: 01/22/01 O: 45.31 H: 45.50 L: 44.25 C: 44.44 Y: 47.37

Prophet Financial Systems, Inc. (www.prophetfinance.com) Used by permission.

In this example, we are confronted with what looks like an ascending or bullish triangle in a downtrend. The strategy to capitalize on the downside breakout is to place a buy stop as marked over $36, the previous rally high before the move out of the triangle. This is a return move after the breakout, but it fails.

THE RECTANGLE

Another continuation pattern you can find if you develop your imagination is the rectangle. (In some older books on chart reading, I have seen this pattern also referred to as a box.) In this pat-

Figure 8.15: A Daily Bar Chart Showing Two Rectangle Formations

Wendys Intl   30.01   0.120   0.401%
D: 07/28/01   O: 17.31   H: 17.37   L: 16.94   C: 16.94   Y: 33.09

Prophet Financial Systems, Inc. (www.prophetfinance.com) Used by permission.

Rectangles are consolidation patterns that appear when the price action is sideways or neutral. Two rectangles can be seen here, along with several flags. The height of the rectangle is projected up or down for an objective.

tern, where prices will fluctuate sideways for weeks or even months, outlining a square or rectangle, the market is stuck between two equally strong support and resistance levels. The height of the rectangle can be used to measure and project a target, just as we did with triangles. See Figure 8.15.

THE RARE DIAMOND PATTERN

The diamond is another pattern that you might encounter. Some analysts consider the diamond a continuation pattern; others view it as a reversal pattern. In either case, there is some agreement that diamond patterns are relatively rare. As a continuation pattern, you might envision the diamond as two back-to-back symmetrical triangles with the first one flipped around. The result is a pattern that first expands and then contracts before breaking out.

Diamonds usually occur in fairly active markets and might look like a couple of head-and-shoulder patterns. (Robert D. Edwards and John Magee, in their classic, *Technical Analysis of Stock Trends*, view the diamond pattern more often as an active top reversal pattern that is easier to identify on weekly charts.) When prices break out of the diamond pattern, they can be projected to travel at least as far from the breakout as the greatest height of the pattern. See Figure 8.16.

Figure 8.16: A Daily Bar Chart with a Diamond Top Formation

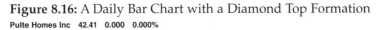

Prophet Financial Systems, Inc. (www.prophetfinance.com) Used by permission.

Here we have the rare diamond pattern as a top reversal. The pattern looks like two triangles that are back to back. Volume is heavy in the diamond, which gives it credibility. In December 2001 and January 2002 we might be forming another diamond, but the volume doesn't support the possible price pattern.

WEDGES

Wedges come in two varieties—rising or falling. Wedges are like triangles in that prices tend to converge, but they are unique in that the trend lines that mark the wedge *both* slope upward or downward. I originally learned to look for wedges as a continuation pattern that may be part of the larger reversal pattern, like a double top or double bottom; but over the years I have also learned to look for wedges to develop as reversal patterns. As continuation patterns, falling wedges usually inhabit uptrends and rising wedges tend to be seen more often toward the ends of declines, and might be part of the first trough of a double bottom pattern.

THE RISING WEDGE

In the rising wedge, both of the trend lines that can outline the formation are slanting upward from the left to the right, but because the two lines tend to converge like a coil, the lower trend line needs to rise at a steeper angle. Volume decreases through the pattern. You might think that the pattern was bullish because both of the lines making up the pattern are rising, suggesting increasing investor interest. Actually, the pattern indicates weaker and weaker interest and a deteriorating technical structure.

In the early stages of a wedge you might mistake it for a channel, but the eventual converging lines of the pattern suggest a point where an apex will halt the advance and a reaction will develop. Prices will extend out to at least the two-thirds point of the pattern and in many cases to the apex or slightly beyond in a "last gasp," but prices typically drop quickly and sharply to retrace all and sometimes more of the advance made during the wedge. See Figure 8.17.

Figure 8.17: A Daily Bar Chart with Volume and a Rising Wedge Pattern

Prophet Financial Systems, Inc. (www.prophetfinance.com) Used by permission.

This 2-month rising wedge formation is a continuation pattern, as the downtrend continues after the pattern. Volume diminishes through the formation and increases on the downside breakout. Notice how prices quickly retrace a large part of the wedge and then eventually all of the wedge. Also note how the top of the wedge becomes resistance that lasts for the rest of the year.

THE FALLING WEDGE

The falling wedge is similar to the rising wedge in its shape and with respect to volume diminishing through the pattern, but falling wedges tend to be found after a long rise. Prices tend to drift downward from a high with converging trend lines. Unlike the rising wedge, where prices quickly retrace their gains, when prices break out of the falling wedge they drift sideways or move in a saucer-like pattern before creeping back up toward the highs. A falling wedge gives you plenty of time and opportunity to reenter from the long side, while the rising wedge is more like a falling knife—you need to recognize it early. See Figure 8.18.

Figure 8.18: A Daily Bar Chart with a Bullish Falling Wedge Pattern

Prophet Financial Systems, Inc. (www.prophetfinance.com) Used by permission.

A 6-week falling wedge formation during May and June breaks out to the upside as a continuation pattern. Typical of falling wedges, it takes a slow four weeks for the wedge to retrace back to its beginning.

INTERPRETING WEDGES

If wedges can be continuation patterns or reversals, how do we recognize the difference? As we mentioned earlier, a rising wedge toward the end of a decline tends to be a continuation pattern that slopes against the trend, and the probabilities favor a downside breakout. A rising wedge seen in an uptrend, with the slope of the pattern in the same direction as the trend, tends to be a reversal pattern and the breakout is most likely downward. A falling wedge is more at home at the end of a rally or near a top, and the pattern is most likely to break out on the upside. A falling wedge in a downtrend tends to be a reversal pattern, with the breakout on the upside. See Figure 8.19.

Figure 8.19: A Daily Bar Chart with Two Rising Wedge Patterns

Amer Express 36.25 0.000 0.000%
D: 01/16/01 O: 47.94 H: 48.94 L: 47.44 C: 48.31 Y: 49.35

Prophet Financial Systems, Inc. (www.prophetfinance.com) Used by permission.

In March–May, we see a rising wedge as a continuation pattern. Once the support at the bottom of the wedge at $34 is broken, the stock plunges. Another rising wedge develops late in 2001, but this turns out to be a reversal instead of a continuation pattern.

TARGETS

The measuring technique for wedges depends on whether they are reversal patterns or continuation patterns. If the wedge is a continuation pattern, the price range of the move prior to the formation of the wedge can be projected from the breakout point, as for the flag and pennant patterns. If the wedge is a reversal pattern, then the distance traveled by the wedge can be projected from the breakout. See Figure 8.20.

Figure 8.20: A Daily Bar Chart with Volume Showing a Rising Wedge as a Reversal

Prophet Financial Systems, Inc. (www.prophetfinance.com) Used by permission.

A rising wedge in April–June marks the end of an advance and the start of a quick reversal. A 2- to 3-month climb is mostly reversed in about two weeks, as the weakness of the wedge becomes apparent.

Gaps: What's Not There Is What's Important

There are six or seven kinds of gaps, but only three are meaningful enough to tell us something important about the supply–demand situation and what to do next. Gaps can show in a very graphic way a sudden shift in supply or demand. As a student of the markets, I have come to realize that most of the time a gap will occur on the supply side for commodities and on the demand side for stocks.

The demand for commodities usually changes slowly with the general level of the economy and personal disposable income, or how much people can afford to spend. Perceptions about the supply of a commodity can change abruptly, and the price is left to sort things out. A gap is really just a price void. Price voids may show up in equities because of a surprisingly good or bad earnings report, a takeover bid, or some other news that causes the stock to gap up or down to adjust more quickly and discount the news. For example, a stock closes at $40.50 with a high for the day of $41.00. The next day the stock gaps up to open at $43.20 and continues to climb, leaving a price gap of $2.20 from $41.00 to $43.20. This price void or gap is bullish until the gap is filled.

WHERE TO FIND GAPS

Gaps are found only on bar charts, candlestick charts, and a few other kinds of charts. Gaps are not found on line charts or point-

and-figure charts. Three gaps are important to understand and watch for: the breakaway gap, the runaway or measuring gap, and the exhaustion gap. Before we examine these three kinds of gaps, let's quickly look at other gaps that have no real meaning for us as we study the market.

GAPS TO IGNORE

The first gap that has no real significance is a gap that represents the minimum price fluctuation for the security in question. In the days when an eighth of a point was the minimum permitted change in the price of a stock, a one-eighth-point gap was meaningless. To have meaning for the technical analyst, a gap must be wider than the changes in price that usually occur.

Other gaps that have no forecasting significance are the ones formed in thin issues during normal trading. If the chart of the issue shows a lot of gaps, then they are not likely to mean anything. Finally, gaps that appear on the charts of stocks when they go ex-dividend do not have any forecasting implications.

Another kind of gap, called a common gap or an area gap, is often discussed with the three significant gaps. The common or area gap appears in triangles and rectangles or other consolidation or continuation patterns and less frequently in reversal formations. So the appearance of gaps in some developing price patterns would tend to reinforce the idea that it will be a continuation pattern rather than a reversal pattern. Thus, the forecasting implications of a common gap are minimal, but they serve some use when you are able to recognize them within a pattern.

HOW WE MEASURE GAPS

A price gap is measured in an uptrend from the highest price on the first day to the lowest price seen on the day of the gap. Gaps are more commonly seen on daily charts, but they can also appear on weekly and even monthly charts. Like any thing else seen on a larger time scale, a gap seen on a chart with a longer time frame is more important technically than one seen on a daily chart.

THE BREAKAWAY GAP

The breakaway gap is the most important gap to recognize, and I think it is the most useful. A breakaway gap typically occurs after a chart pattern has been completed, and usually indicates the beginning of a major price move. Breakaway gaps usually occur on heavier than normal volume and they usually are not filled. In the case of an upside breakaway gap, prices may trade down to the upper end of the gap and may even dip halfway into the gap, but some amount of the gap is typically left unfilled—as a kind of constant reminder of the breakout. There are two other generalizations to keep in mind about breakaway gaps. First, traders believe that the heavier the volume on the day of the gap, the more likely the issue is going to keep climbing and the less likely you will see any kind of pullback. A downside breakaway gap from a top pattern may or may not occur on heavy volume, but it tends to be less important. Keep in mind the old expression: "It takes volume to move a stock up, but it can fall of its own weight." Second, after a breakaway gap appears, it is not unusual for a stock or other security to make other gaps as traders jump on the new trend. See Figures 9.1 and 9.2.

THE RUNAWAY GAP

Gaps that occur in the course of an uptrend or downtrend are called runaway gaps. Most of the time, seasoned traders prefer to wait for a reaction or correction to buy or sell a security. The pullback, bounce, or retracement often gives you a lower-risk entry point for positions. But sometimes a stock can keep moving, with the advance or decline accelerating. When this happens, traders will jump on to buy out of fear of missing the boat. A gap that occurs in this manner is a runaway gap.

Figure 9.1: A Daily Bar Chart with a Breakaway Gap to the Upside

Circuit City Strs-crctctygrp   20.34   0.340   1.21%

Prophet Financial Systems, Inc. (*www.prophetfinance.com*) Used by permission.

Circuit City breaks out of a 7-month consolidation pattern with a breakaway gap on the upside. Volume expands to confirm the move up, and the stock doesn't look back until it makes a triple from the September low of just $10. There was still a lot of money to be made if you bought on the day of the gap.

Figure 9.2: A Daily Bar Chart with a Breakaway Gap to the Downside

Inco Ltd   16.97   0.140   0.832%
D: 01/18/01   O: 15.55   H: 15.55   L: 14.80   C: 14.96   Y: 18.67

Prophet Financial Systems, Inc. (*www.prophetfinance.com*) Used by permission.

Not all breakaway gaps are bullish. Here Inco Ltd trades sideways for two to three months between $18 and $16, making a rectangle formation. The stock breaks the support at $16 and gaps downward, even breaking old support above $14. Gaps can also be found on the upswing in the stock in October and November.

Runaway gaps are also called measuring gaps. These gaps tend to occur in the middle of a move up or down. If you can measure the length of the move to the gap, you can project it away from the gap to get a price target. See Figure 9.3.

Figure 9.3: A Daily Bar Chart with Gaps

Contex Corp   53.20   0.510   0.968%
D: 01/19/01   O: 39.88   H: 39.88   L: 38.00   C: 38.50   Y: 60.00

Prophet Financial Systems, Inc. (www.prophetfinance.com) Used by permission.

The doubling of Centex from its September low leaves a few gaps in its wake., The third gap near $48 in early December is called a runaway gap. The length of the immediate rally of $7 from $40 is repeated after the gap, as the stock climbs to reach $57 from $49.

THE EXHAUSTION GAP

The last kind of gap that carries significance is the exhaustion gap. (See island reversals in Chapter 7.) As a trend comes close to its end, an exhaustion gap can form on relatively light volume. This gap is filled very quickly, and it tells you that the bulls or the bears that have been running the market up or down are through. The exhaustion gap tends to be created by buyers in an uptrend or sellers in a downtrend recognizing and joining the trend very late. The last people to come on board, these late buyers or sellers tend to be weak in that their financial resources are limited. They create that last surge, but when the market fills the gap they created they are quick to bail out of their longs or cover their shorts. Their actions accelerate the trend in the opposite direction. See Figure 9.4.

Figure 9.4: A Daily Bar Chart with an Exhaustion Gap

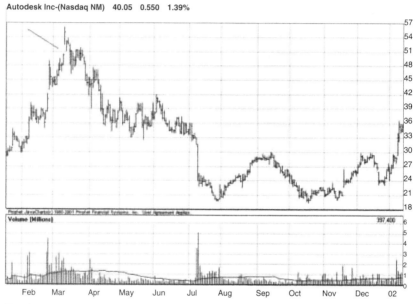

Prophet Financial Systems, Inc. (www.prophetfinance.com) Used by permission.

Autodesk sprints from $30 to nearly $57 in about six weeks. Volume expands rapidly, supporting the move, but the spike day to nearly $57 leaves behind a gap. This gap is filled quickly, making it an exhaustion gap. The gap up may have been formed by short sellers covering or late buyers jumping in, but the gap represents the exhaustion of the move up.

GAPS AS PART OF ISLAND REVERSALS

An exhaustion gap is often the first gap made in an island reversal. The second gap in the island will be a breakaway gap in the other direction. In between these two gaps, the market or the security holds for a few days in a tight range, almost as if it has paused before the next move. That next move comes soon enough, as the security reverses direction, leaving that 3- or 4- or 5-day pattern isolated from the rest of the price action by the gaps. If you use your imagination, you can see the island.

HOW TO TRADE GAPS

You might think that trading gaps is useless, but in some markets it can be critical for getting into a strong position. When you are confronted with a breakaway gap or a runaway gap in an uptrend, don't panic. Take a moment to collect your thoughts and get paper and pencil. The first thing to do is write down the high of the previous day and the opening price of day two; the difference is the gap and it is only a number.

There are times when the news that created the gap is so dramatic that prices continue trading higher and higher, never looking down again. But there are also times when prices surge higher and are hit with a wave of profit-taking. This could come from traders who bought yesterday and want to take the quick profit, or traders who bought the opening and are now nervous and want to sell. This early selling sometimes creates a dip that can extend halfway into the gap.

FIND THE HALFWAY POINT

Take that piece of paper with the initial gap written on it and determine the halfway point. The dip into the gap tends to be fast and unreliable. If you are trying to get long, the best approach is to use scale-down buy orders. At every $1/8$th or 32nd point or every penny lower, layer your orders to buy from the top of the gap to the midpoint. If the breakaway gap is valid, you should not fill the gap entirely, and a new round of buying should develop to push the market back up. You may not get everything bought that you hoped for, but if you remember this approach you won't panic.

There is an old expression, "All gaps must be filled." I don't know where this expression came from, but if you follow that saying you might be making one of the most costly market mistakes. The important gaps are created because there is a dramatic change in supply or demand. While some gaps may eventually be filled as future events unfold, there are probably gaps on stocks from 1929 that have yet to be filled. I can remember gaps on silver charts when the market peaked at $50 an ounce in early 1980. It can be dangerous to your financial health to be waiting for those gaps to be filled. A gap can occur because of a structural change in the market or some other reason that reflects an underlying shift. There is no sound reason to expect that these gaps should ever be filled. If you were using a point-and-figure chart in those cases, the question of gaps would not even come up.

GAPS ON CANDLESTICK CHARTS

Gaps appear on candlestick charts, but the candlestick chartist commonly refers to a gap as a "window." A window is the gap or price void between the prior day's and the current day's price extremes. The candle approach expects that corrections will go back to a window. The window acts as support in an uptrend and resistance in a downtrend. The lower shadows of the candlestick patterns can fill the window, and that is okay. The trend remains positive until you have a close below the window. Longs should be liquidated or sold and shorts should be considered if the selling continues after the window has been filled. The reverse action occurs with windows in downtrends. The windows act as resistance until a close above the window. See Figures 9.5 and 9.6.

Gaps can be very informative. Once you decide what kind of gap it is and how you want to react or respond to it, don't hesitate because the gap is a dramatic way of telling you something has changed.

Figure 9.5: A Daily Candlestick Chart with Gap as Support

Parker Drilling   3.59   -0.009   -0.277%

An upside gap or window acts as support for the stock during October, November, and December. Prices dip into the gap, which is allowed, but we do not close below the gap. Notice how the rallies have failed at old resistance around $4.10.

Figure 9.6: A Daily Candlestick Chart with Gap as Resistance

Newmont Mining Corp Inc New   20.36   0.410   2.06%
D: 07/16/01   O: 18.87   H: 18.96   L: 18.30   C: 18.50   Y: 24.65

Around mid-November, Newmont Mining gaps down and breaks a 3½-month uptrend line in the process. For the next eight weeks, the bottom of the window or gap acts as resistance on rallies.

Draw Your Own Trend Lines and Channels

You learned about basic trend lines in Chapter 4. Here we want to explore drawing lines parallel to the basic trend lines to form channels. This chapter is relatively brief, but the technique is very important and should be examined closely. Channels develop more often than you think, and can provide you with great trading opportunities.

When you examine enough charts you will find that prices often become trapped in a channel between two parallel lines. One of these lines is the uptrend line or the downtrend line, and the other line is the channel or return line. Channels can also be found in sideways or trendless periods when prices move laterally between a support line and a resistance line.

Trend lines can be used for spotting turns early with channels and return lines, when the price action in a downtrend fails to reach the return line that runs parallel to the downtrend line. This can be an early warning that the trend is shifting from down to sideways and perhaps even up. If you are looking at an upward-sloping channel and the rallies above the uptrend line stop short of the parallel return line, this may indicate that the market is running out of upside momentum. See Figure 10.1.

Figure 10.1: A Weekly Bar Chart with a Downward-Sloping Channel

Timken Co   16.60   -0.059   -0.359%

Prophet Financial Systems, Inc. (www.prophetfinance.com) Used by permission.

The major down channel on Timken gives one several trading opportunities from both the long and short sides. The failure to even come close to the return line of the channel in September 2001 is an early warning that the trend is turning sideways to up.

WHAT DEFINES A CHANNEL?

The minimum you need to see for a tentative uptrend channel is two lows with an intervening high, followed by a rise above the intervening high, giving validity to the second low. This is shown in Figure 10.2.

For a downtrend channel, the minimum you need is two highs with an intervening low, followed by a fall below the intervening low, giving validity to the second high.

As soon as these conditions are in place, you can draw a trend line (up or down) and a tentative channel line or return line that is parallel to the trend line. Once these trend lines and return lines are in place, you want to see a second peak in an up channel or a second trough in a down channel to confirm or validate the channel. Figure 10.3 shows a valid channel.

Figure 10.2: A Daily Line Chart Showing the Three Points Needed to Draw a Channel

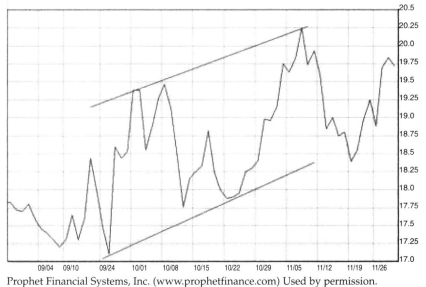

Prophet Financial Systems, Inc. (www.prophetfinance.com) Used by permission.

This simple line chart shows the minimum three points needed to draw a channel. More points touching the lines give greater validity to the channel.

Figure 10.3: A Daily Bar Chart with a Valid Channel

Prophet Financial Systems, Inc. (www.prophetfinance.com) Used by permission.

The upward channel gets validity in November on the upside and downside with successful tests of the return line and the uptrend line.

Just as we follow and may adjust trend lines over the course of a major move up or down, we also want to redraw the channel or return line when the trend line is redrawn.

HOW TO PROFIT FROM CHANNELS

Channels can be very profitable for active traders. Long positions can be initiated at the uptrend line and profits can be taken at the return line as long as it remains in force. The reverse can be done in down channels, with traders buying against the return line and selling on approach to the downtrend line. See Figure 10.4.

Figure 10.4: A Weekly Line Chart Showing a Sideways Channel

Asa Ltd   21.80   0.700   3.32%

Prophet Financial Systems, Inc. (www.prophetfinance.com) Used by permission.

For more than three years, you could have traded ASA Ltd back and forth in this neutral or sideways channel. A breakout over $22 is going to look very bullish if it ever happens.

WATCH FOR EARLY SIGNALS

Trend lines and channels can be used to gain subtle clues about possible reversals or shifts in the trend. If you have drawn a valid uptrend channel and prices do not decline back to the uptrend line and begin to rally again, it can mean that prices are beginning to accelerate to the upside and a new, steeper trend may have begun. See Figure 10.5.

The reverse image would be seeing a rally in a valid down channel failing to reach the downtrend line. If the rally stops sooner than expected, it can mean the technical condition of the stock or market has weakened and the move down may become nasty.

Figure 10.5: A Daily Bar Chart with an Upward-Sloping Channel

Wendys Intl   30.20   0.190   0.633%

Prophet Financial Systems, Inc. (www.prophetfinance.com) Used by permission.

This chart shows the stock running out of momentum. The rallies in November and January for Wendys fail to reach the return line of the channel. The stock is still in a good uptrend and holding support, but we have an early warning that the bulls need to rest.

CHANNELS AS INDICATORS OF TURNS

Channels can be used as leading indicators of turns when they fail to reach the return line or channel line. The failure to reach the channel line is the wake-up call. In an upward-sloping channel, prices could still hold the uptrend line and trade higher within the channel. Prices need to break the uptrend line to warrant a change in trend from up to sideways. If a lower low and lower high are made after the failure to reach the channel line, then a downtrend has been established. See Figure 10.6.

In a downward sloping channel, if we fail to see prices touch the return line, it is an early tip-off that the downtrend has

Figure 10.6: A Daily Bar Chart with Channel Breakdown

Agnico Eagle Mines   11.08   0.380   3.55%

Prophet Financial Systems, Inc. (www.prophetfinance.com) Used by permission.

Another great-looking channel in which the stock runs out of steam in November. The stock gaps down and breaks the uptrend line. The failure in early November to extend the rally to the underside of the return line with a big outside day and a lower close was an early clue that the stock could weaken.

Figure 10.7: A Daily Bar Chart with Channel and RSI

Prophet Financial Systems, Inc. (www.prophetfinance.com) Used by permission.

Adding the action of the 14-day Relative Strength Index, we can see how weak the early November rally was, failing to cross back above the 70 threshold.

slowed and a sideways trend or even an uptrend could be next. Look again at Figure 10.1, then at Figure 10.7.

PRICE TARGETS

Much like the price patterns we have covered in earlier chapters, channels have measuring implications. In all the bar chart patterns we looked at we have measured the vertical height of the pattern and then extended it on the upside or downside. With channels, once you have a breakout from the channel, the market will usually move a distance that is equal to the width of the channel. All you have to do is measure the channel and project that distance above or below whichever trend line is broken. See Figure 10.8.

Figure 10.8: A Daily Bar Chart with Channel Breakout and Measurement

Prophet Financial Systems, Inc. (www.prophetfinance.com) Used by permission.

Ryder trades for three months in a bull channel and then breaks out on the upside. How far can the rally carry? Measure the height of the channel, here about $2, and then add it to the breakout point on the upside, here giving us a target at $24.

TRADING CHANNELS

If you want to trade a channel successfully, I recommend adding an overbought/oversold indicator to the chart (see Chapter 14 for a fuller discussion). In this way, you can get some confirmation, when prices touch the trend line or the channel line, as to whether the market will rebound from the line or possibly break through. See Figure 10.9 and revisit Figure 10.7.

You can easily see that channels are a powerful tool for trading and getting an early tip-off for a potential trend change, so take the time to look for them and apply them.

Figure 10.9: A Weekly Bar Chart with Channel and Slow Stochastic

Prophet Financial Systems, Inc. (www.prophetfinance.com) Used by permission.

The failure of the XAU to touch the return line of the down channel in November is accompanied by an oversold buy signal on the slow stochastic indicator. This turns out to be foreshadowing the rally through the top of the downtrend line.

Moving Averages
Smooth Things Out

In previous chapters we looked at subjective tools. To use them, you had to decide where and how to draw the trend line or what price pattern, if any, you might be looking at. Is it a triangle or a wedge? How do you measure the pattern for a price objective? Where is the tallest point? Like other skills, some people grasp these ideas easily and excel, while others struggle. In addition, in time everyone falls prey to the false pattern or false breakout, as well as making other errors in judgment. To me, these are not reasons to abandon subjective tools; but to others, these drawbacks have provided impetus to find and create more objective approaches that can be programmed and tested.

In this chapter, we look at mathematical trends—smoothed, simple, and weighted. Moving averages have been applied to the financial markets for at least 50 years; they belong to a category of indicators called trend-following indicators.

TREND-FOLLOWING INDICATORS VERSUS OSCILLATORS

Trend-following indicators are meant to smooth out prices so a trend can be seen as a line, making it easier to find the beginning and the end of a trend. Trend-following indicators lag or follow the price action. They tend to be useful in trending markets and to give poor results or even losses in sideways markets.

Moving averages form the basis for many of today's mechanical trend-following systems. The other major indicators are momentum oscillators or overbought/oversold oscillators, and they are covered in Chapters 14, 15, and 16. Price momentum can be measured and can show us when the speed of price change is slowing and a reversal might be near. These indicators tend to lead or be coincident to the turns in the market.

How Moving Averages Have Changed

Moving averages are probably among the oldest ways of analyzing prices. They have evolved over the past 50 years from simple to weighted, to exponential, and to something called adaptive. Buy and sell signals have changed over the years from simple closes above or below the moving average to multiple crossovers with additional conditions. Instead of charting the price of the stock or commodity directly, we are charting the average closing price for a number of time periods. We are removed from the direct price action and are plotting a line that is a representation of the trend of prices. The smoothing makes it easier to see the trend, but we are a step removed from the pure price action.

What Do We Average?

The close or settlement price is usually used in calculating the moving average, but you could just as well average the highs or the lows or the range of trading for the day. A compromise approach might be used—take the midpoint value, the range of the day divided by two. You could also add the high, low, and closing prices, and divide by three. Moving averages can be run for the highs and the lows separately, giving us an envelope around the price action. In addition, moving average envelopes set at a percentage above and below the moving average can act like smoothed channels in giving you trading signals.

THE SIMPLE MOVING AVERAGE

The first moving average we look at is the simple arithmetic moving average. This is the most commonly used type of average. It treats all the data in the same way. The approach itself is simple, too. Add up the number of hours or days or weeks under question, and then divide by that number. The average "moves" by adding a new item and subtracting the oldest item. The new total is divided again by your parameter—10, 20, 50 days, and so on.

By averaging the data over some period of time, erratic price changes are smoothed out and the underlying trend can be seen more clearly. If you had trouble drawing trend lines in Chapter 10, then perhaps moving averages are better suited for you. Even if you are good at spotting trends and drawing trend lines, the signals given by the more widely followed moving averages should not be ignored. Table 11.1 shows how a moving average is calculated.

Table 11.1: Calculating a Simple Moving Average

PRICE	5-DAY TOTAL	MOVING AVERAGE
$101		
$100		
$103		
$ 99		
$ 96	499	99.8

Applying Logic

When I began my career in the commodities market, I was taught that the moving average you used or applied should make some logical sense. It made sense that a 4-week moving average was applied to weekly data, or a 12-month moving average to monthly data. But there were other applications. The application of the 200-day moving average on stocks dates back at least to the late 1950s and maybe earlier.

I was taught that the 200-day moving average was applied to the price of silver because that was the annual silver requirement of Kodak, a major consumer of silver. The 200-day moving average of Handy and Harmon's spot price of silver was used in monitoring and adjusting Kodak's silver inventory—not quite a year's worth of data. If silver prices were below the 200-day moving average, Kodak supposedly ran down its inventory because it could replace it with cheaper material. If the price was above the 200-day moving average and sales were good, the company would consider extending coverage through purchases of the cash commodity or futures, depending on its sales forecast and the price outlook for silver.

I once visited the purchasing department of Lever Brothers. I found that they tracked a 4-month moving average on soybean oil because, I was told, four months was the shelf life of margarine. This is another example of the use of a logical moving average.

Naturally, there are other moving average periods that make sense. The 5-day moving average represents a week and the 21-day average represents a month of trading. A quarter of a year is 13 weeks, a half-year is 26 weeks, and a 12-month moving average makes sense for looking at a lot of long-term data. The strongest reason to follow a moving average that is based on logic is that it should always work. A moving average that may have worked well in the past may not work in the future, under different conditions. A logic-based moving average should work as well going forward as it does backward.

MATCH THE LENGTH TO THE TREND

In addition to using moving average lengths that are logical, lengths should be matched to the trend you desire to follow:

- Very short-term market trends should be tracked with moving averages that are from 4 to 13 days in length.
- Short-term market trends should be tracked with averages that span 14 to 25 days.
- Minor intermediate-term trends can be tracked using moving averages of from 26 to 49 days.
- Intermediate-term trends can be tracked with averages of from 50 to 100 days.
- Long-term trends are best tracked with averages that range from 100 to 200 days in length.

DRAWBACKS TO SIMPLE MOVING AVERAGES

The simple moving average has two major drawbacks that have prompted analysts to look for other approaches. The first problem is that the moving average covers only the time period being averaged, whether it is 10 days or 50 days or 200 days. Earlier data may be important, but it is dropped off as the average moves. The second complaint by analysts is that equal consideration is given to each price, when it can easily be argued that more recent prices are more important and should be given more weight in the average, as opposed to a price from 50 days ago. In answer to these complaints, weighted moving averages and exponential moving averages were developed.

THE LINEARLY WEIGHTED MOVING AVERAGE

With a linearly weighted moving average, greater weight is given to the more recent closing prices. A 10-day weighted moving average multiples the tenth day by 10 and the ninth day by 9 and the eighth day by 8, and so forth. The total is added up and divided by the sum of all the multipliers (10 + 9 + 8 + 7 + 6 + 5 + 4 + 3 + 2 + 1, for a total of 55). This method takes care of the problem of equal weighting, but it does not address the so-called drop-off effect. The exponentially smoothed moving average handles both problems.

THE EXPONENTIAL MOVING AVERAGE

While exponential smoothing might seem more complicated than the simple or weighted moving average techniques, it is simply another weighted moving average. Fans of exponential smoothing believe the approach is simple to calculate in that only the last exponentially smoothed value (Et-1) and the smoothing constant a are needed to figure out the new value. (Interestingly, the technique seems to date back to World War II, when it was used as a way of tracking aircraft and projecting their positions.)

$$Et = Et-1 + a\ (Pt - Et -1)$$

New
exponential = Prior
value exponential +
value + Some % of $\left(\begin{matrix} \text{today's} \\ \text{price} \end{matrix} - \begin{matrix} \text{prior} \\ \text{exponential} \\ \text{value} \end{matrix}\right)$

An important feature of the exponentially smoothed moving average is that all the data that were previously used are always part of the new outcome, but with less and less significance. (This is how the complaint about data dropping off in the other moving averages is addressed.)

SIGNALS

Calculations are one thing, but useful signals are quite another item. We now have a clear, smooth line displaying the trend. How do we make use of it? We'll look at one moving average, then two averages, and finally a three-moving-average system. Each system has its benefits and drawbacks; you must decide how complicated you want to make things.

THE 1-MOVING-AVERAGE SYSTEM

The idea behind the single moving average is that in an uptrend, the moving average tends to lag the price action and trails below the prices. When the uptrend comes to an end and a downtrend develops, the price should move below the moving average. The trading rules from this simple observation are easily derived:

- Go long when the price of the security crosses from below to above the moving average line.
- Go short when the price of the security crosses from above to below the moving average line. See Figure 11.1.

Figure 11.1: A 15-Day Simple Moving Average

Intl Business Machines   118.03   -0.0199   -0.016%
D: 01/16/01   O: 93.75   H: 94.00   L: 91.01   C: 92.75   Y: 87.48

Prophet Financial Systems, Inc. (www.prophetfinance.com) Used by permission.

The 15-day simple moving average of the daily closes of IBM is shown here. While the stock does trend nicely at times, you can still see periods where there are repeated whipsaws.*

DRAWBACKS

The trading rules listed earlier essentially mean you are always in the market, either long or short, depending on whether prices are above or below the moving average. The main drawback to this method is that you will have losses on consecutive transactions when the market is in a trading range and prices swing back and forth around a moving average. So, almost by definition, trend-following indicators like moving averages are money losers in a trading-range market.

WHICH CHART TO USE

Because the closing price is commonly used to calculate a simple moving average, does it mean that a close-only chart is the best

---

*Whipsaws are repeated, sharp trend reversals that cause most trend-following and breakout systems to give you a string of losses.

chart to overlay the moving average on? This would be the most logical conclusion and would give you signals on the close, but our two trading rules say to open and close positions as the price crosses the moving average. What do we do if we overlay the moving average on a vertical bar chart? See Figure 11.2.

Figure 11.2: A 10-Day Simple Moving Average

IBM-Intl Business Machines MA(10)

Prophet Financial Systems, Inc. (www.prophetfinance.com) Used by permission.

A 10-day simple moving average of the daily closes of IBM hugs the price action even closer than the 15-day average shown in Figure 11.1. If you decide to use an intraday break of the moving average, you get a lot of signals in the October–November rally. Compare this to Figure 11.3.

When we look at a bar chart with a short-term moving average overlay, we find many more times when prices violate the moving average. If we took every one of the price violations as a trading signal, we would find trading this trend to be impractical and unprofitable, while it is profitable using a line chart. See Figure 11.3.

Figure 11.3: A Daily Line Chart with a 10-Day Simple Moving Average

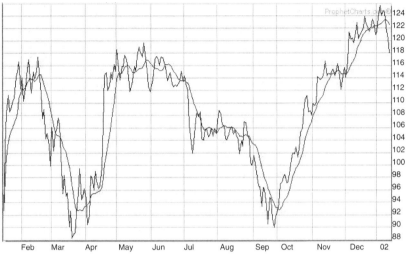

IBM-Intl Business Machines MA(10)

Prophet Financial Systems, Inc. (www.prophetfinance.com) Used by permission.

This is a 10-day simple moving average of the daily closes of IBM against a line chart. With this approach, there are fewer signals in the October–November advance. Compare this to the whipsaws in Figure 11.2.

TIME ADJUSTMENTS

Technicians have come up with two ways to handle the problem of receiving too many signals from a moving average. One way is to adjust the length of the moving average so that only significant price violations are given. This usually means lengthening the moving average, which typically results in later buy and sell signals as the trend turns up and down. This also gives rise to a separate problem with moving averages. If we shorten the time frame of the average, it becomes more responsive to price but we are whipsawed more often with short-term buys and sells. If we lengthen the time frame, we get fewer whipsaws but the signals are late.

SIGNAL ADJUSTMENTS

Another way to deal with intraday price violations is to add on various filters that need to be fulfilled before a trade is signaled. Some of the more common filters used in intraday moving average crossovers are:

- *Close:* The price must close above or below the moving average.
- *Entire Bar:* An entire bar must trade beyond the moving average, the high, and the low.
- *Percentage:* The price must cross the moving average by a certain percentage of the price of the moving average.
- *Price Units:* The price must cross the moving average by a certain number of price units.
- *Time:* The price must cross the moving average by a certain time period—two days, three days, or a week.

The more sophisticated technique is to use the direction of the moving average line alone or in combination with the five filters listed. Because we are smoothing the price so we can see the trend better, we find that there are three possible trend situations:

1. The moving average line is rising and we are in an uptrend.
2. The moving average line is falling and we are in a downtrend.
3. The moving average line is flat and there is no trend or a narrow trading range.

If we use the direction of the moving average as a filter on a crossover, then we will be long only when the moving average is moving up, and be short only when the moving average line is moving down. This also means that you are out or aside from the market when the moving average line is flat. (We'll look at using momentum oscillators to trade nontrending markets in Chapter 14.) But remember, the direction of the line is not used by itself, but as a filter when prices cross the moving average.

THE 2-MOVING-AVERAGES SYSTEM

Another approach to handling the problem of defining when the price crosses the moving average line (beside using filters) is to use two moving averages. A moving average with a short time window is used in place of the actual price line, combined with another moving average that represents the underlying trend. The 2-moving-averages approach has been popular among professional money managers and advisors for many years.

Different combinations can be used, but consider the logic behind this example. A common fast-moving average is the 5-day average. It's a short cycle and also represents the trading week. (Some people consider four days a short time frame for a moving average and use 4-day in combination with 9-day and 18-day moving averages.) Once you decide on the fast moving average to represent price, then a slower moving average needs to be selected to identify the trend. The 21-day moving average can be used for the trend identifier and makes some logical sense as the number of business days in a month. When we bring the two moving averages together on one chart, we can see how the trading rules apply. See Figure 11.4.

- A *buy* signal occurs when the fast moving average crosses from below to above the slower moving average.
- A *sell* signal occurs when the fast moving average crosses below the slower moving average.

Similar to a single moving average, using two moving averages will still give poor results when a trading range develops and good results when prices are trending, either up or down.

Make an Oscillator

Another application of the 2-moving-averages system is to move the information to the bottom of the graph and show the mathematical difference between the two moving averages as an oscillator. An oscillator is an indicator designed to measure whether a market is overbought or oversold. The oscillator is very easy to

Figure 11.4: A Daily Bar Chart with 5-Day and 21-Day Simple Moving Averages

IBM-Intl Business Machines MA(10)

Prophet Financial Systems, Inc. (www.prophetfinance.com) Used by permission.

The 5-day average is very quick and represents a week of data. The 21-day moving average is slower and corresponds to a month of trading. Go long when the 5-day crosses over the 21-day, and go short when the 5-day crosses under the 21-day. Using this approach, a trader would have captured the bulk of the rally from $98 to $122.

construct. All you have to do is subtract the moving average for the longer time span from the average for the shorter one. The results can be plotted as a line chart and are normally displayed along the bottom, so the peaks and troughs can be compared to the price action above.

The oscillator can be used in two ways. First, we can get overbought and oversold signals when the short-term moving

Figure 11.5: Two Moving Averages Displayed as an Oscillator

Prophet Financial Systems, Inc. (www.prophetfinance.com) Used by permission.

The difference between two moving averages can be used as an over-bought/oversold indicator. When a security gets too far above the longer moving average, it is overbought and due for a correction.

average has advanced too fast and too far above the longer-term average. These readings may only mark a temporary pause in the trend, as a consolidation or continuation pattern may develop to unwind the overbought or oversold condition.

Second, as the oscillator travels or crosses back and forth over the zero line, buy and sell signals are given. When the oscillator crosses above zero, buy or go long; when it crosses below zero, sell or go short. See Figure 11.5.

THE 3-MOVING-AVERAGES SYSTEM

While the 1- and 2-moving average systems may represent an improvement in generating clearer buy and sell signals, they connote that one is always in the market and either long or short.

Unfortunately, these systems do not tell you when you should be out of the market—for example, during choppy sideways periods when signals are generating a string of losses and you begin to doubt the wisdom of this method. Technicians developed the 3-moving-averages system as a way to address this problem. Let's first look at three ways to select time windows for the three moving averages, and next we'll look at the entry rules.

CYCLE LENGTHS

The first approach to selecting a time frame is to use three consecutive cycle lengths. In the equity arena this could be a 5-day moving average representing a week, a 21-day average for a month, and a 63-day average representing a quarter. In the commodity markets, the 4-, 9-, and 18-day averages are commonly used. This system also appears as a slightly faster version of the 5-, 10-, and 20-day moving average numbers, which leads us into the next approach.

HARMONIC NUMBERS

Another method is to use harmonic numbers, such that each cycle length is related to its neighboring cycle. This means that the next longer or next shorter cycle length is related by a factor of two. The monthly cycle is probably the best-known cycle in the commodity markets. If we take 20 days as the monthly cycle, then 40 days is double, 10 days is half, and 5 days is half again.

FIBONACCI NUMBERS

Using the early part of the Fibonacci number series (1, 1, 2, 3, 5, 8, 13, 21, 34, 55) is another method. Some analysts use a 5-day, 13-day, and 34-day moving average combination. Note that the 21-day moving average is a Fibonacci number. Of course, other moving average combinations might be used after back-testing over historical data.

TRADING RULES

The trading rules for the 3-moving-averages system hinge on the idea that all three averages will be in a desired formation in markets that are trending strongly higher or lower. When the moving averages are not in the right pattern, then you stay out of the market. The moving averages must be in a long mode before going long. The long mode is when the shortest moving average crosses above the medium moving average, and the medium moving average crosses above the longest moving average. See Figure 11.6.

The short or sell mode occurs when the shortest moving average has crossed below the medium moving average, and the medium average has crossed below the longest average.

Figure 11.6: The 3-Moving-Averages System

IBM-Intl Business Machines MA(10) MA(20) MA(30)

Prophet Financial Systems, Inc. (www.prophetfinance.com) Used by permission.

Take another look at IBM with the 10-, 20-, and 30-day moving averages. A buy signal does not occur until the 10-day crosses above the 20-day, *and* the 20-day crosses above the 30-day. You are out of the market for half of October, and you don't go long until about $102. You have fewer whipsaws, but you do not catch the bottom of the move.

The exit rules for a 3-moving-averages system are not a mirror image of the entry signals. A long position is closed out or liquidated as soon as the fastest moving average has declined below the next fastest moving average.

Once this signal has been given and acted upon, stay out of the market until the market moves to either a setup for a short mode or a new long mode. A short position or trade would be covered as soon as the fastest moving average crosses to above the next fastest moving average. Again, stay out of the market until either the moving averages turn up to generate a long trade, or the market turns down again to a short mode.

GRANVILLE'S RULES

Before we end our discussion of moving averages, we should take a look at Joseph Granville's eight basic rules for interpreting the 200-day moving average in his book *New Strategy of Daily Stock Market Timing for Maximum Profit*.

1. If the 200-day moving average turns flat or rises after a decline, and the price of the security brekas the moving average line on the upside, this is a key buy signal.
2. If the price of the security breaks under the average while the line is still advancing, this too is a buy signal.
3. If the security is above the 200-day line and dips toward it and turns up again, this is also a buy signal.
4. If the stock price falls quickly below a falling average line, you might get a short-term rebound.
5. If the average flattens out or declines after a rise, and the security breaks that line on the downside, this is your key sell signal.
6. Another sell signal comes if the price of the security rises above the line while the line is still falling.
7. If the security is below the average line and rises toward it, and turns down again, this is also a sell signal.
8. If the security rises too fast above a rising moving average line, you can sometimes anticipate a reaction.

The 200-day moving is not a sensitive indicator, and trend reversals are likely to be outlined in the price action well before the moving average turns down or up.

USE MOVING AVERAGES WITH CONFIDENCE

Moving averages, no matter which you use, are straightforward in their calculation and should have a place in your style of trading or investing. They can be tested and can aid in your money management approach. With today's computing power and software, there is no need to shy away from even the most complicated methods. Just think logically and use discipline.

Using Relative Strength
for Selection

Relative strength (RS) seems to be one of the oldest approaches within the field of technical analysis, and is widely used in the equity arena, even among people who would never classify themselves as technical analysts. The narrow definition of relative strength compares at the price action of an individual stock or a group of stocks to the market as a whole, usually defined as the Standard & Poor's 500 (S&P 500). With RS we are trying to see if the stock or group is acting better or worse than the broad market. We can also examine the performance of one group compared to another group, such as capital goods and consumer goods.

While one might argue successfully that absolute performance is the only true measure of a money manager, relative performance is probably used more than any other approach to evaluate money and managers. In the final analysis, if you are doing better than your competitor or your peer group, that's what counts. You can lose money, but as long as you lose less money than everyone else, it's okay.

A BRIEF PROFILE

The study of relative strength by some parts of the academic community helped to refute the popular random walk theory, also known as the Efficient Market Hypothesis. In the latter part of the 1960s, published research showed that stocks that performed well continued to perform well, and that stocks that performed poorly continued to perform poorly. More recently, studies by Lowry's Reports, Inc., of North Palm Beach, Florida, have shown

Figure 12.1: Investment Returns from the Groups with Better Relative Strength Readings

For comparison purposes, also assume that each week an investor bought equal dollar amounts of the Industry Groups that are included in the table of *Industry Groups* showing *Weak* Power Rating Returns. The chart below shows the results of this study:

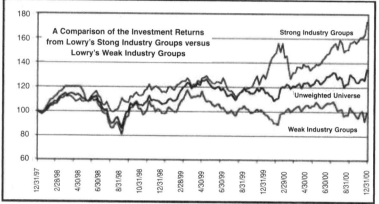

Lowry's Reports, Inc. Used by permission.

This chart is a graphic display of the results over a 3-year period of investing in the strongest groups compared to the weakest groups, using the relative strength of the group as the determining factor.

"that concentrating stock purchases with the Industry Groups that reflect the strongest investor buying enthusiasm can dramatically enhance overall investment performance."

RS even works in futures pits with very short-term traders. Successful local traders buy strength and sell weakness. Spreaders in the pits operate in the same way, by buying the strongest month or commodity and selling the weaker month or commodity. See Figure 12.1.

CALCULATING AND HANDLING RELATIVE STRENGTH

Today, many different methods can be used to calculate relative strength. The most common and simplest approach is to divide the daily or weekly close of a stock or a group by a market average or index; most often the S&P 500 is used in the case of equities.

Relative strength can also be used to look at intermarket relationships. We could look at a ratio of bond futures to gold futures to see if financial assets were doing better than tangibles or vice versa. We could look at gold and oil in a ratio. Of course, the stocks-to-bonds ratio is important for market timing in asset allocation.

How about the ratio of the Nikkei 225 to the S&P 500 or some other stock index? Is the Japanese market outperforming, or is the U.S. market? Where should we put our money? Are emerging markets starting to outperform?

By looking at simple RS charts, you can make better decisions about where to place your assets. The stock, group, sector, economy, or region that shows the best RS should command more of your investment dollars. See Figures 12.2 and 12.3.

Figure 12.2: Wendys Compared to the S&P 500, Daily Bar Chart with Relative Strength

Prophet Financial Systems, Inc. (www.prophetfinance.com) Used by permission.

Throughout 2001, this stock outperformed the S&P 500 index by a wide margin. Notice the dramatic outperformance from April through September. From September, Wendys still rises, but the S&P 500 is catching up and the relative performance is flat.

Figure 12.3: Agnico Eagle Mines Compared to the S&P 500, Daily
Chart with Relative Strength

Prophet Financial Systems, Inc. (www.prophetfinance.com) Used by permission.

This gold mining stock doubled in price, while the S&P 500 came
under pressure in the first half of 2001. AEM outperformed relatively
and absolutely compared to the index. The S&P 500 has caught up a
bit since the second half of September.

ANALYZING RELATIVE STRENGTH

There are a number of ways to analyze relative strength. You
could look for divergences or to see if something is "out of gear,"
but using RS is a more subtle approach. For an analysis of the RS
line, you can use trend lines, moving averages, momentum,
price patterns, and even support and resistance. Like momentum (see Chapter 14), the RS line usually reverses ahead of the
trend in the index. All these methods of examining the RS line
are useful and can add value, but it is important to identify the
major trend in the market. You don't want to pick a stock with a
rising RS line just because the S&P 500 was falling faster because
this means you are losing money slower than the average.

MORE WAYS TO LOOK AT RELATIVE STRENGTH

Other approaches some analysts have used are to look at the level of the RS index and the price index itself, including volume. In a rising trend you would want to see the RS line rise and confirm the move up. If the index rose to three new highs while the RS failed to make a new high on the third rally, it would suggest a negative or bearish divergence. This would mean that the trend of the index was likely to change to the downside. The opposite can occur at lows, with the index making three successive lows and the RS line making two new lows but failing for some reason to make a third new low. This divergence in a move down is known as a positive divergence and would suggest that the index or stock could display good upside leadership after a bottom.

Volume is a confirming indicator, and it can be used as such with the RS line. A stock that is moving up on increased volume is good. The expansion of volume tells you that more buyers have been attracted to the uptrend. If we saw an uptrend with rising volume and a divergence with the RS line, it would suggest that, despite the rise in the stock price and good participation, the stock was not rising as fast as the general market. See Figure 12.4.

Figure 12.4: Table of Results from Lowry's Reports, Inc.

Summary of Results:	
Annual Rate of Return from Investing in Industry Groups showing **Strong** Power Rating Patterns	**+20.34%**
Annual Rate of Return from Investing in Industry Groups showing **Weak** Power Rating Patterns	**–0.31%**
Annual Rate of Return from Buy-and-Hold Investment in Lowrey's Unweighted Primary Universe Index	**+10.49%**
Annual Rate of Return from Buy-and-Hold Investment in Standard & Poor's 500 Index	**+11.22%**
Period covered: 3 years Dec. 1997 — Dec. 2000	

Lowry's Reports Inc. Used by permission.
This table shows that the best returns come from investing in the strongest groups.

We know that Relative Strength is an accepted method for selecting stocks that might be screened by fundamental criteria before being included in a portfolio. Today, one brokerage house has a mutual fund that was established to follow its technical analysis department's model portfolio, which is weighted by the groups' performance. Groups that have better RS get an over-weighting of money.

HOW TO APPLY RELATIVE STRENGTH

As you look for investment ideas, check the RS of the sector or industry you are interested in. Ask yourself if it is stronger than the S&P 500. If the answer is yes, it will mean that institutional money could be moving in or will be attracted going forward.

Once you have identified the stronger groups, look for the individual stocks that show the best RS lines within the group. You want to single out the best of the best. After you have compiled a short list of stocks that are outperforming their peers and the averages, zero in by looking for the stock with the best risk–reward setup. (See Chapter 19.)

Getting Confirmation
with Volume

Volume is the second piece of data that comes from the market-place. If the marketplace produces only two basic pieces of infor-mation—price and volume—why is it that we are more than halfway through this book before we discuss volume in detail? The obvious answer, often overlooked, is that people don't buy and sell at a particular volume figure. People buy and sell price and are most interested in prices.

Technical analysis tends to focus on price above everything else: how price reflects the psychology of the marketplace, how it plays out on the chart in the various patterns we have covered, and how one price relates to another price in intermarket analy-sis or relative strength.

A seasoned technical analyst once told me that if volume indicated something important and you acted on this knowl-edge in the marketplace, your actions would show up in the price. Thus, the most important piece of data is the price, and the thing to watch is the price action. Given that understanding, vol-ume is a great confirming indicator, and you should use it when-ever possible. Surely, anything that can confirm a price pattern or help interpret the strength of a trend will be a welcome addi-tion to your technical work. However, good, accurate, real-time volume figures are not known for every market, and this means you should use price as the first and foremost tool of analysis.

In the bank currency markets and the cash bond market, real-time volume figures are not available, but that situation is changing with a growing percentage of currencies and bonds being traded on-line or reported by companies like GovPx.

TWO WAYS TO FOLLOW VOLUME

There are two ways to analyze volume, and it is wise to explore both of them. First, volume can be followed visually at the bottom of a chart (except in point-and-figure and Equivolume charting). We will discuss some generalizations about what volume is forecasting in the following section. The second approach is driven by math, with some underlining assumptions about how markets work. For about 40 years now, traders and analysts armed with calculators and computers have attacked volume in various ways. We will discuss some of these methods in the section headed "Applying Math to Volume."

VOLUME PRECEDES PRICE

Volume tends to mirror the price action, but a lot of research has found that volume leads prices. In research done in the late 1960s and in the 1980s, the peak in volume has led major price peaks by approximately nine months on average. (Interest rates also lead stock prices at major turns by approximately nine months on average, so a peak in rates and interest-rate-sensitive stocks may be the key here.) The results of this research should not be hard to grasp. Remember what we learned about head-and-shoulder tops in Chapter 6? The heaviest volume of the pattern is seen in the left shoulder, and each of the following rallies should see lower and lower volume. After the left shoulder, the head goes on to make a new high for the move up, so the final price high in the market average or stock tends to occur after the volume high. Naturally, all stocks don't peak at the same time, and of course a head-and-shoulders pattern won't develop on every one of them, but this goes to the heart of the explanation of why trading volume peaks before the final price high in the major averages.

Analysts who examine volume as a leading indicator usually measure the rate of change of the volume, comparing it to a recent time period; or they may use a moving average of the volume figures to smooth them. Analysts use these approaches because volume is a relative concept. Researchers have found that, historically, the rate of change in volume led the rate of change in price. The results were better for bottoms.

WHAT TO WATCH

If we accept that volume tends to lead price, what exactly do we look for? In a strong or healthy uptrend, the volume of trading tends to expand with rising prices and contract with declining prices. The same rule is true in downtrends: Volume increases on the downdrafts and declines on the countertrend or short-covering rallies or bounces. This is what we expect to see in a normal trend development, and it does not alert you to danger or a reversal of trend. Besides confirming an advance or decline, volume can alert you to trouble ahead. See Figure 13.1.

Figure 13.1: A 1-Year Daily Bar Chart with Volume

Prophet Financial Systems, Inc. (www.prophetfinance.com) Used by permission.

BJ Services has heavy volume on the late-September selling climax and it begins a fourth-quarter rally. Volume diminishes through the rally, telling you the uptrend is weak. The uptrend line is broken and the stock breaks lower.

VOLUME IN TRENDS

Remembering the discussion of top patterns, if we have a rally to a new high and volume expands but is less than the volume seen on the prior rally, then we should be on alert for a possible trend reversal. Also, rallies that continue on diminishing volume lack committed participation and should be monitored for a potential price reversal. See Figures 13.2 and 13.3.

If you see high volume develop with no further upward price progress after an advance, it is usually a bearish signal. This indicates that, despite good buying pressure, there was an equal amount of selling pressure to stymie the price advance. On the downside, if you find high volume with no price weakness after a decline, it is usually a bullish signal. Some traders also watch for volume to dry up at a low after a downtrend. They believe that this lull in volume means the market is "all sold out" and you should be alert for a rally. See Figure 13.4.

Figure 13.2: A 2-Year Daily Bar Chart with Volume

Prophet Financial Systems, Inc. (www.prophetfinance.com) Used by permission.

Volume is very light throughout the base pattern in 2000. A small double bottom in November 2000 is the start of a good advance. An uptrend takes hold with volume increasing on each rally and diminishing on the sideways consolidations.

Figure 13.3: A 6-Month Daily Bar Chart with Volume

Textron Inc   40.69   0.060   0.148%
D: 07/19/01   O: 55.24   H: 55.55   L: 54.99   C: 55.28   Y: 22.29

Prophet Financial Systems, Inc. (www.prophetfinance.com) Used by permission.

Look at the upward-sloping channel with the failure to reach the return line in January. If you combine this with the flat volume picture, it leads you to expect that the 2½-month uptrend line on TXT will be broken and probably will find support at $36.

Figure 13.4: A 6-Month Daily Bar Chart with Volume

Pride International(delaware)   12.58   0.480   3.97%
D: 07/18/01   O: 40.05   H: 40.42   L: 39.67   C: 40.03   Y: 18.39

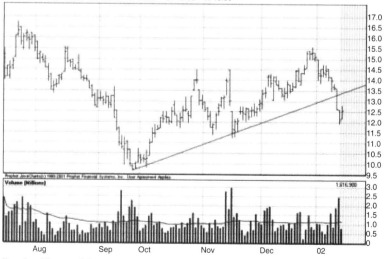

Prophet Financial Systems, Inc. (www.prophetfinance.com) Used by permission.

Here is another example of a weak uptrend. Volume expands a little on some of the small rallies, but overall the volume declines from November to December to January. Note how volume really increases on the break of the uptrend line in January 2002. The stock has retraced 50% of the rally, so it may hold and rebase around $12.

VOLUME ON BREAKOUTS

Even if you haven't yet looked at enough charts to get used to watching for subtle clues from volume shifts, you should still be able to notice volume on breakouts from patterns. They should be very clear on the chart. Volume is very important at breakouts and will confirm the breakout *if volume increases significantly*. A breakout on light volume is questionable first of all, and could be a false move up or down, but it is also a tip-off of a possible return move to the breakout point.

Volume is important for the proper interpretation of price patterns. Some years ago, a number of technicians and traders in the fixed income market eyed a possible head-and-shoulders top pattern. Nearly everyone was bearish and they all saw the same,

Figure 13.5: A 5-Year Weekly Bar Chart Volume

General Electric 38.71 0.810 2.14%
D: 03/03/97 O: 16.83 H: 17.47 L: 16.71 C: 17.39 Y: 47.54

Prophet Financial Systems, Inc. (www.prophetfinance.com) Used by permission.

In the bull market decade of the 1990s, everyone wanted to buy GE on weakness. See how volume expands into the October 1998 low and is low in the first quarter of 2000. The game changes in 2001. Jack Welch steps down as CEO and the volume is now increasing on the decline—despite the spike low at $30, the 50% retracement, the stock is still in a downtrend.

potentially bearish, top pattern outlined in the prices, with the same neckline. I wasn't convinced. The outline of a head-and-shoulders pattern in price was correct, but the volume levels did not decrease through the formation. I doubted that the pattern was a valid head-and-shoulders top and I looked for other confirming indicators. I did not find anything else to support my contention that the price pattern was a continuation pattern and not a top reversal, but all the technical studies were price-based. I stuck my neck out with my company's clients and my peers. Fortunately for the clients who followed my advice, and for the sake of my reputation as an analyst, the pattern was not a head-and-shoulders top formation, and the bonds did in fact continue to rally to new highs. See Figures 13.5 and 13.6.

Figure 13.6: A 10-Year Monthly Log Chart with Volume

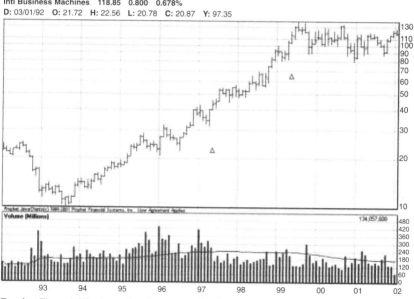

Prophet Financial Systems, Inc. (www.prophetfinance.com) Used by permission.

As IBM recreated itself in the middle to late 1990s, investors poured into the stock; volume swelled and the stock rose steadily. Volume peaked in early 1997, but the stock continued to climb. During 2001 the stock traded up close to a breakout, but volume did not confirm the move. Is another setback in order?

APPLYING MATH TO VOLUME

For decades, volume analysis was only visual and rather subjective. Typically, we looked at the price chart and the histogram or vertical bars of the volume at the bottom of the chart. Like looking for a price pattern, our eyes became trained to look at whether volume was rising or falling. All the guidelines in the past for using volume were basically generalizations, not hard-and-fast rules. In the early 1960s, analysts began to display and combine volume and price in many new directions, first by hand calculations, and then using computers.

ON-BALANCE VOLUME (OBV)

While some research notes suggest that as early as 1948 an approach similar to on-balance volume (OBV) was used, Joseph Granville appears linked to the method since the early 1960s. On-balance volume is cumulative volume, or simply a running total of volume. If today's close is higher than yesterday's close, you add today's volume to the cumulative or running volume total. If today's close is lower than yesterday's close, you subtract the period's volume from the running total. If you get a day with no change in price, the volume is ignored or passed over and the running total remains unchanged from the previous day. Each day you add or subtract the volume numbers, and the cumulative total is plotted as a line indicator and compared to the price action of the security. See Figure 13.7.

The level of the OBV line is not important in the analysis, in that the level depends on when you start adding the figures. The direction of the line and the pattern it makes at tops and bottoms when compared to the price action are important. We know that volume often precedes price action, so OBV can move before prices and the OBV line can be considered a leading indicator. A rising OBV line confirms an uptrend, and the OBV line should trend lower if prices are in a downtrend. When the price of the security and the OBV line are both making higher peaks and troughs, the uptrend is likely to continue. When the price and the OBV line are both making lower peaks and lower troughs, the downtrend is likely to continue. A divergence between the

Figure 13.7: A 2-Year Daily Bar Chart with the On-Balance-Volume Study

General Electric 38.71 0.810 2.14%
D: 01/18/00 O: 49.38 H: 49.38 L: 48.43 C: 48.84 Y: 61.60

Prophet Financial Systems, Inc. (www.prophetfinance.com) Used by permission.

The downtrend in GE may go on for a while longer because the on-balance volume line has been confirming the price action. The OBV line needs to diverge from the bearish price action to give us some hope for a recovery on this favorite.

OBV line and the price can be a signal for a price reversal. Because Granville believed that volume preceded price, he theorized that the OBV line could show evidence of accumulation or distribution. See Figure 13.8 (next page).

Granville reasoned that if prices were going sideways and the OBV line was rising, it meant that so-called smart money was buying or accumulating ahead of a price rise. When the upside breakout came, the OBV line would continue to rise with prices as the public jumped on board. If prices were trading sideways and the OBV line was falling, it would be a sign of distribution. Smart money was liquidating their positions or distributing stock before a price decline. When the down move gets under way, the OBV line will continue to drop as the general public gets out of their holdings.

Figure 13.8: A 9-Month Daily Bar Chart with the On-Balance-Volume Study

Inco Ltd 16.88   0.050   0.297%
D: 04/17/01   O: 16.24   H: 16.66   L: 15.90   C: 16.64   Y: 17.83

Prophet Financial Systems, Inc. (www.prophetfinance.com) Used by permission.

Granville's on-balance volume (OBV) line is confirming the October–November advance, and peaked in early December. The stock needs to set a new high, with the OBV line also making a new high, to confirm the price action.

Granville extended the study of OBV from individual stocks to the major averages and even to the most-active list. Several publications and Web sites list the top 10, 15, or 20 most active stocks, and an OBV line can be constructed with just these issues being added together. Because the most-active list can represent a significant part of the total volume, divergences between the most-active OBV line and the DJIA can point out some worthwhile turning points. Be wary if the DJIA makes new highs but the most-active stocks OBV line doesn't confirm the price action. This lack of commitment shown in the volume figures is a warning.

Even though the original OBV line continues to be used by analysts and traders nearly 40 years later, some analysts found Granville's approach too simple. If a stock spent most of the day trading lower and closed up by only one-eighth of a point, why should all of the volume of the day be added to the cumulative total? One adjustment to Granville's OBV approach is the Volume

Accumulator by Mark Chaiken. Instead of lumping all the volume to either the buyers or the sellers, Chaiken decided to assign a proportion of the volume in a way that expressed the relationship of the close to the intraday price mean. If prices closed at the extreme high or low of the day, then all the volume would be added or subtracted. If the close was at the middle of the range for the day, then no volume was added, unlike Granville's system. The formula for the Volume Accumulator is as follows:

$$\text{VA today} = \text{VA previous} + \left(\frac{\text{Close} - \text{Low}}{\text{High} - \text{Low}} - .50\right) \times 2 \times \text{Volume}$$

Other approaches have been tried, such as applying volume to the percentage price change from close to close or smoothing out the daily volume numbers. Some traders like to give greater weight to strongly trending days; this can be done by multiplying the volume by the amount of the price gain. See Figure 13.9.

Figure 13.9: A 2-Year Weekly Bar Chart with 10-Week Rate of Change of Volume

Inco Ltd   16.88   0.050   0.297%
D: 01/25/99   O: 11.31   H: 11.50   L: 10.44   C: 10.56   Y: 24.21

Prophet Financial Systems, Inc. (www.prophetfinance.com) Used by permission.

Here we have a 10-week rate of change study on volume. From 1999 to the end of 2000, we mostly see the rate of change of volume increase on rallies; but in 2002 there is a subtle change, and the rate of change is positive on the declines. The big question is whether this foreshadows the breaking of the downtrend.

UPSIDE AND DOWNSIDE VOLUME

When analyzing the stock market as a whole, or using what is known as the top-down approach, researchers have looked at the volume in advancing stocks and the volume in declining stocks separately. Looking at upside and downside volume is a way of attempting to forecast whether the market is undergoing accumulation or distribution.

One popular way of looking at upside and downside volume is by cumulating the difference between the daily volume, in millions of shares, between the advancing stocks and the declining stocks. This plurality can be cumulated and plotted as a line. Similar to OBV, upside and downside volume plotting can be started at any time and at any arbitrary number. However, because you can be subtracting some large numbers, it would be better to pick a high starting point so you won't be generating negative numbers on your chart. Similar to other techniques we have looked at, the upside and downside line can be plotted below the price index, and you will look for divergences. A rise in the index to a new high that is not matched by the upside and downside volume index moving to a new high is a warning sign for a downside reversal. Moving averages and simple trend line analysis can be applied to the upside and downside volume line to spot turning points.

PROBLEMS WITH FUTURES

At the beginning of this chapter, we mentioned that real-time volume is not available for every market. The futures market in the United States is one example. For the moment, the majority of commodity trading in the United States is still conducted by the open outcry method on the floors of the various exchanges. Depending on the market, there might be 600 to 700 or more people in the pit. From this sea of shouting traders, we try to get price and volume information. The exchanges employ pit reporters to record the price changes in the pit and transmit them to traders around the world through their terminals and computers. An estimate of volume is also made by the exchange and reported by most of the markets on a half-hourly basis throughout the trading day.

These estimates are pretty good, but they are not disseminated quickly during the day, and the actual cleared total volume figures are not reported until the next day. The only people who have a good idea how much was traded at a particular price are the floor traders and the clerks close to the ring. This is part of the "edge" the local floor trader has over the upstairs trader. The floor trader knows whether the new high in price was made on a small 10-lot order or on 500 contracts from a broker who handles business for a large trading house that deals in the physical commodity.

Tick Volume as an Alternative

Tick volume isn't perfect information, but it is the next best thing to being on the floor. Tick volume is a reasonable substitute for actual volume. Simply stated, tick volume is the number of price changes in a given time interval. In a 5-minute period in the bond futures market, we might see prices change rapidly 200 times between 100-10 and 100-12 (par and 10/32nds and par and 12/32nds). We don't know the sizes of the orders but we assume the market is busier and has traded more volume than if prices changed only twice in five minutes. This is a similar concept to point-and-figure charting (see Chapter 3). We don't record the volume (nor the time) with point-and-figure charts, but we can reasonably assume that the volume of trading probably increases with the price activity on the chart.

Tick volume can be used like OBV, and short-term divergences can help you spot intraday price highs and lows. A move to a new intraday high in price that is not accompanied by a new high in tick volume is suspect, and a decline is possible. On the downside, a new low in price that is not accompanied by a new low in tick volume is an indication the market oversold on a short-term basis and a bounce is possible.

One method I found successful with bond futures is to take a 6-period moving average of the 5-minute tick data and make something similar to an OBV line. If futures closed up at the end of the 5-minute period, the tick number was added; it was subtracted if prices declined. The data was smoothed out but the approach was the same—to spot bullish and bearish divergences. The technique was to look at a 5-minute bar or candlestick chart with the smoothed OBV line of tick volume below it. A new low in price on the bar chart that was not matched by a new low on the tick volume suggested the move down was running out of steam. A new intraday high that did not get a corresponding new high from the smoothed tick volume line was likely to fail.

Use this combination of tools to day trade instruments like bond futures, or to refine the timing of entry of a longer-term trade.

The Ups and Downs
of Oscillators

Aside from the calculation of moving averages, our discussions of technical analysis so far have been very subjective—interpreting chart patterns, drawing trend lines, finding support and resistance areas, and so on. Now we are going to concentrate on indicators based on price; not price directly, but prices indirectly—mathematical constructs that are derivatives of prices. While one might think that these indicators can add clarity and precision to technical analysis, overreliance on them can actually lead to mistakes in trading and investing.

Moving averages are meant to smooth the price action, similar to trend lines. But there are other indicators, like momentum oscillators, that are meant to help you in trading-range markets and to give you *advance warning* of a change in trend. Moving averages can help identify a change in trend only *after* it has taken place.

Momentum oscillators or indicators can often tell you something about the underlying strength or weakness of the market through the indicator. Please note that we interchange the words oscillator and indicator frequently. While there are some indicators that do not fluctuate or oscillate, the word *oscillator* is often substituted for the word *indicator*, and the opposite also occurs.

Some users of technical analysis start to believe that because these indicators are covered in later chapters and use math, they are more advanced and therefore superior. This incorrect image is kept alive in magazine articles and advertisements, and even by some professional market technicians who are trying to show the superior results from their favorite indicator. I don't believe the application and use of an indicator should be placed ahead of the price action on the chart. The indicator should be a secondary tool to help clarify and understand the price action. While people do trade on signals from indicators, people can only buy and sell price in the marketplace. The price action on the chart should come first and should be given priority when you are trying to decide what to do.

KEEP YOUR EYE ON PRICES

Relying on an indicator for the trading signals without paying attention to the price action may be the biggest reason so-called successful trading systems don't live up to their advertisements. I can't tell you how many times I have read or heard, "The market is oversold and you should go long; buy it"; "I've never seen the market so oversold"; "This market is as overbought as 1987; we have to go down." All of these comments and strategies are dangerous. If you should go long the market because it is oversold using an indicator, without seeing some sort of reversal pattern on a chart, you run the risk of the market going lower and getting even more oversold. In addition, there are countless examples of the market trading sideways instead of going into an expected rally to relieve oversold readings. Unless you have a special option trade, tying your money up in a sideways market is not what you want to do. We'll discuss overbought and oversold situations in greater detail after we talk about momentum.

Some indicators are designed to lead the price action; others are coincident; and some are late or lag the price action. If you use indicators that lead the price action, extra time must be taken to wait for the price action. If an indicator says the market is due to rise or fall, become prepared for that kind of reaction, but do not get ahead of the price action. Always remember two things: (1) No investment technique is perfect. (2) Traders deal in probabilities, not certainties.

MOMENTUM OSCILLATORS

One category of oscillator that technicians have polished over the years is the momentum oscillator. These oscillators are used to measure the speed or direction of price change. Just as you could throw a ball in the air, and with the proper tools, measure the speed at which it travels, we can look at the rate of price change using the correct oscillator. Gravity will slow the speed of the ball thrown in the air until it stops rising and begins to turn down. The rate of change in prices will also slow and turn down before the final price high. See Figure 14.1.

Figure 14.1: A 5-Year Weekly Bar Chart with 10-Week Rate of Change

Prophet Financial Systems, Inc. (www.prophetfinance.com) Used by permission.

During 1999 and early 2000, the S&P 500 climbed to new record highs, but the 10-week rate of change made lower highs and the peak in the ROC study preceded the peak in prices.

BASIC PRICE MOMENTUM

You can easily get lost with complicated oscillators, because their construction and the logic they are based on may be the exception rather than the norm, so we'll start with one of the most basic measures—momentum. As we've said, momentum measures the rate of change or the velocity of price changes. We are not concerned with the level of prices. Price momentum is measured by continually taking the price differences for some fixed time interval. A 1-day momentum oscillator subtracts yesterday's price from the latest price. A 10-day momentum oscillator subtracts the closing price 10 days ago from the last closing price. The result, which could be positive or negative, is plotted around a "zero line." The formula for a price momentum oscillator is simple:

$$M = V - Vx$$

where V is the closing price and Vx is the closing price x days ago. As with moving averages, the shorter the time period selected, the more sensitive the oscillator.

We noted in Chapter 11 that moving averages are trend-following indicators that work best in trending markets and could give many unprofitable signals in a trading-range market. Momentum oscillators can be used to trade the swings within trends, and they can alert you to a change of trend. These oscillators might be considered the most useful in trading-range markets, where tools like moving averages don't react quickly enough.

Moving averages are late by definition, so when you follow their signals, you can get long at the top of the move and short at the bottom. Moving averages are often drawn over the price chart, while oscillators are usually drawn in a separate chart displayed below the price chart.

We mentioned that a momentum oscillator swings back and forth around a "zero line." This is true for the vast majority of oscillators, but some oscillators can be constructed to move back and forth within established boundaries, such as between 0 and 100. Setting boundaries can make it easier to know what the extreme levels are, but other problems can develop.

CALCULATION

Let's look more closely at how the formula for momentum works. See Figures 14.2 and 14.3.

When a move up or down starts to develop, volume expands (confirmation of the move) as more traders and investors want to get on board, so the rate of change or momentum increases. As a rally or decline matures, more and more investors have satisfied their buying or selling needs, and the amount by which prices move in each period (usually a day) tend to decrease. Let's look at some simple longhand examples to see how this works.

If today's price is $70 and yesterday's price was $65, then the 1-day momentum is $70 − $65 = 5. The price has a rate of change of $5 per day. If today's price is $70 and the price five

Figure 14.2: A 5-Year Weekly Bar Chart with 12-Week Momentum Study

Prophet Financial Systems, Inc. (www.prophetfinance.com) Used by permission.

In the steep price slide of the S&P 500 in 2001, a 12-week momentum study confirmed the decline. No bullish divergences are evident. Prices made a new low and so did the indicator.

Figure 14.3: A 1-Year Daily Bar Chart with a 20-Period Momentum Study

IBM-Intl Business Machines

Prophet Financial Systems, Inc. (www.prophetfinance.com) Used by permission.

A 20-period momentum study on IBM points out an interesting divergence in late 2001. IBM has a steep markup or rally, but the 20-day momentum peaks and diverges from the price action halfway through the advance. Prices begin to react lower in early 2002.

days ago was $60, then the 5-day rate of change or momentum is $70–$60 = 10. The security is moving at a rate of $10 in five days, or $2 per day. A simple table and some charts will show how momentum will peak before the price high.

DATE	PRICE	1-DAY MOMENTUM
Sep 4	$ 70	
Sep 5	$ 72	72 – 70 = 2
Sep 6	$ 74	74 – 72 = 2
Sep 7	$ 78	78 – 74 = 4
Sep 10	$ 83	83 – 78 = 5
Sep 11	$ 90	90 – 83 = 7
Sep 12	$100	100 – 90 = 10
Sep 13	$108	108 – 100 = 8
Sep 14	$115	115 – 108 = 7
Sep 17	$120	120 – 115 = 5
Sep 18	$123	123 – 120 = 3
Sep 19	$124	124 – 123 = 1

You can see how momentum hits its peak at 10 on September 12, when prices reach $100. Prices continue to rise, but the momentum decreases. Momentum peaks before the price high at $124. This makes momentum a leading indicator because it can alert us to changes in direction before they occur. Prices could go sideways after peaking, but let's see what momentum does when prices stop rising and begin to decline.

DATE	PRICE	1-DAY MOMENTUM
Sep 20	$124	124 – 124 = 0
Sep 21	$122	122 – 124 = –2
Sep 24	$119	119 – 122 = –3
Sep 25	$114	114 –119 = –5
Sep 26	$106	106 – 114 = –8
Sep 27	$ 99	99 – 106 = –7
Sep 28	$ 95	95 –99 = –4
Oct 1	$ 93	93 – 95 = –2
Oct 2	$ 93	93 – 93 = 0

The extreme low in momentum was –8, when prices declined to $106 on September 26. Prices continued to decline and then flattened out. An analogy is a car slowing down to make a turn. If we are tracking the speed of the car, we can probably anticipate when the car will turn by the reduced speed of the vehicle as it slows ahead of the turn.

OVERBOUGHT AND OVERSOLD INDICATORS

Now that we have a sense of momentum, we need to understand two well-worn technical terms—overbought and oversold. We know that prices can either trend or be at rest. When prices are at rest, or at equilibrium, they don't exactly stand still. Prices tend to move sideways in a trading range when they don't trend. Rather than waiting for prices to break out and begin a trend, we can use tools to trade these range markets. We need tools to tell us when each up and down move is completed so we can sell our longs and go short or cover our shorts and go long. We know when we look at a trading-range market that no rally or decline will last very long, and that momentum will reach levels at which we can anticipate turning points. We get the terms *overbought* and *oversold* from the levels where the momentum peaks or troughs.

A stock or other financial instrument is overbought at the price level that coincides with the extreme levels of a momentum oscillator above the zero line around which the oscillator swings. On the downside, a stock or other security is oversold at the price level that matches up with the extreme levels of a momentum oscillator below the zero line.

Although some technical analysis books and Web sites may use particular levels on an oscillator as "lines in the sand" for their trading signals, you would be better off thinking about overbought and oversold conditions as zones or ranges that can shift upward or downward in a bull or bear phase. We know that oscillators can be set up to swing above and below a zero line, or we can make them stay within a preset range, so this gives us two ways to establish overbought and oversold levels.

When a momentum oscillator is designed to fluctuate between 0 and 100, for example, then technicians have assigned levels that are considered overbought and oversold. Typically, the levels of 70 and 30 or 80 and 20 are assigned as points deemed overbought and oversold. When a momentum indicator is calculated without upper or lower boundaries, we must look backward on the chart from right to left to see what levels marked previous extremes in the prices. Neither of these approaches should be considered inflexible, because they are somewhat subjective in that market structure can change.

In the late 1970s, when everyone was flocking to gold and silver, the markets became overbought and they stayed overbought. Oscillator readings were in the 90s as the market was pushed higher and higher without a break. If you got out of a long position or went short because the market was so overbought, it was an expensive experience.

The other thing to remember is that the market can make a sea change. For years it may trade in a broad sideways market, but then something may ignite a huge rally. All those years of sideways markets will have you expecting this advance to fail quickly, but the past is only a guide to the future. A market can enter a period of such sustained price strength that all the prior data can be tossed aside.

Figure 14.4: A 1-Year Daily Bar Chart with a 20-Period Momentum Study

PDE-Pride International(delaware)

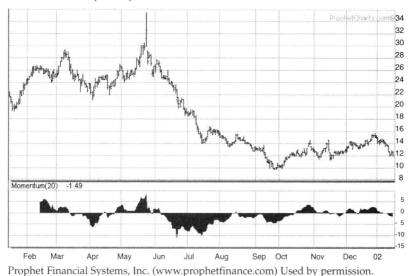

Prophet Financial Systems, Inc. (www.prophetfinance.com) Used by permission.

Pride International (PDE) rallies 50%, from $10 to over $15, and tests key resistance in the $15 to $16 area. A 20-bar momentum study does not confirm the new highs for the move up in December, and prices stall and weaken in the beginning of 2002.

In addition to the signals given by extreme readings, the crossing of the zero line can give you trading signals on the direction of the trend. A crossing above the zero line is a buy signal and a crossing below the line is a sell signal, as long as these buy and sell signals were taken in uptrends or downtrends. See Figure 14.4.

FINDING DIVERGENCES WILL IMPROVE YOUR TRADES

No discussion of signals from oscillators is complete without a discussion of divergence. A divergence occurs when the price series makes a new high or a new low and the oscillator does not make a new high or low. This divergence from the momentum oscillator tells you that even though the prices have continued to rise or fall, the momentum or rate of change was not as strong as in the previous move up or down. This failure to make a new high or low in the momentum study tells you the bulls or the bears are losing their commitment to the trend in force. See Figure 14.5.

Although you may get a divergence from the momentum indicator, that does not mean you should immediately take a position in the market. When you spot a divergence, get confirmation from the price index. This confirmation could come in the form of a trend line being broken, a close above or below a key moving average, or the completion of a price pattern like a head-and-shoulders top. Why wait for confirmation? First, con-

Figure 14.5: A 3-Year Weekly Bar Chart with a 13-Week Momentum Study

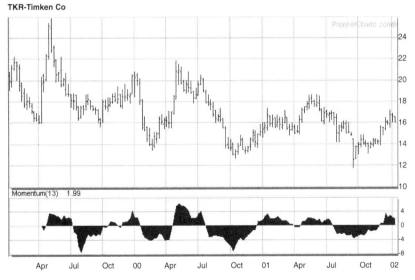

TKR-Timken Co

Prophet Financial Systems, Inc. (www.prophetfinance.com) Used by permission.

In this example, we find a bullish divergence from the move down on Timken in late September 2001. The new lows in price are not accompanied by new lows in the 13-day momentum study. A rally over the $18 to $19 area is what we should be looking for on TKR.

Figure 14.6: A Futures Chart and a 13-Day Momentum Study

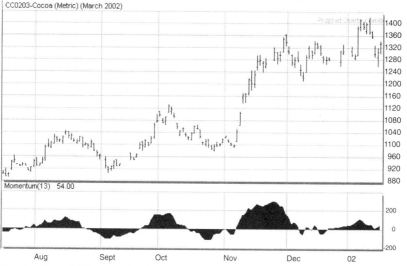

Prophet Financial Systems, Inc. (www.prophetfinance.com) Used by permission.

A possible, glaring, bearish divergence is seen between the new highs in January 2002 and the lower high on the 13-day momentum study in the same month. There isn't enough evidence just yet, but the suggestion is to wait for the market to decline back to major support at $1,200.

firmation of a turn up or down will help tilt the odds in your favor when you trade or invest. Second, in a major trend, a stock can gain or lose momentum without breaking the trend. With any confirmation signals, some subjective analysis is involved; if you thought that oscillators would make technical analysis more objective, we are sorry to disappoint you. See Figure 14.6.

There are some other rules to keep in mind when using oscillators. One is similar to a rule for using trend line tests and areas of support and resistance: The more bearish divergences you get in an uptrend, the weaker the trend. Conversely, the more bullish divergences you find in a downtrend, the stronger the reversal or base that is developing. Another observation is that at the beginning of a strong uptrend, the overbought readings don't generate much of a decline. They are similar to a reverse signal that shows how strong the move is—it gets overbought and still keeps rising. When a trend is fairly mature (such as a bull move longer than three years), another clue to watch for is a strong move in the momentum oscillator with only a tepid move in the price. In that case, despite strong momentum, the price structure is weak.

TYPES OF DIVERGENCES

We know that prices can trace out many patterns, and we can also outline a number of types of divergences. The type of divergence that probably gives the best signals occurs when the price makes a lower low and the oscillator makes a higher low. This is the classic bullish divergence. The classic bearish divergence occurs when prices make a new high and the oscillator makes a lower high. (A bullish divergence means prices will turn higher, and a bearish divergence means that prices should turn lower.) See Figure 14.7.

Figure 14.7: A 9-Month Daily Bar Chart and a 12-Day Momentum Study

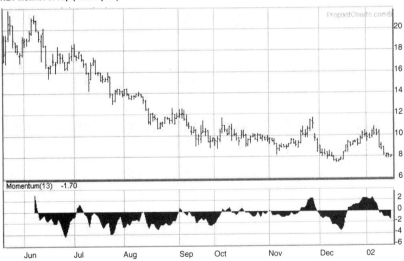

INET-Instinet Group-(Nasdaq SC)

Prophet Financial Systems, Inc. (www.prophetfinance.com) Used by permission.

Prices are moving lower in early 2002, but the 13-day momentum is not making a new low for the move down, so beware of a firmer market ahead.

Another kind of divergence can be seen in double tops and double bottoms. In this divergence, prices make an equal low, but the oscillator makes a higher low. On the upside, prices could make equal highs or tops while the oscillator made a lower high.

The last kind of divergence you will encounter occurs when prices make a lower low but the oscillator makes an equal low. On the upside, the converse is seen with prices making higher highs, but the oscillator making equal highs.

The occurrence of a bullish or bearish divergence doesn't mean that prices have to reverse. Like almost everything else we look at in technical analysis, confirmation is needed. How do we get confirmation and improve the results? As noted earlier, if you see a bullish or bearish divergence without some trend-reversal signal, it would be wise to wait for a signal before taking a position. If you see a divergence after you see signals of a trend reversal, then the divergence is an additional confirming indicator.

15

What's So Special About RSI?

Don't confuse the Relative Strength Index with the relative strength analysis of stocks discussed in Chapter 12. The Relative Strength Index (RSI), developed by J. Welles Wilder Jr., is a way of measuring price momentum that is a little different and a little more difficult to calculate than a simple momentum study. RSI has been around for about 30 years and has become very popular with technicians and with the general investing public. RSI is probably found on every financial Web site that has a charting application. Compared to other measures of overbought and oversold conditions, RSI gives clearer signals and absolute levels. From trader to trader in the United States or abroad, there is little confusion by what is meant when someone says "The 9-day RSI is up at 74."

HOW TO CONSTRUCT THE RSI

The formula for RSI is pretty straightforward:

$$RSI = 100 - \frac{(100)}{(1+RS)}$$

where $RS = \dfrac{\text{Average of } x \text{ days up closes}}{\text{Average of } x \text{ days down closes}}$

Wilder used 14 days in his original calculation because it was one-half of the 28-day cycle that had been observed in the commodity markets. A 9-day RSI has become very popular and is the usual default on many systems and Web sites. Many traders who use the 4-, 9-, and 18-day moving averages system are also fond of using the 9-day measure of RSI.

RSI is set to fluctuate from zero (0) to 100, so overbought and oversold levels are generally set at 70 and 30, respectively. Over the years, many analysts and traders have noticed that there is an upward bias to the numbers, so that in a bull market, the overbought indicator should be 80 instead of 70.

Another observation people have made is that corrections to the downside in bull markets tend to be shallow, often not pulling back as far as you thought they could pull back. The reason this happens is that people want to buy to get into the stock or index. They are excited about the upside and are probably less patient traders, so they start buying earlier on the correction than investors might. To adjust for this, consider the 40 area and below on the RSI as oversold in a bull market. If you keep the 30 or even 20 level in mind for your buy signals, then you are likely to miss the dip. For downtrends in bear markets, use the 60 level as overbought, because sellers will come in before the market gets overbought to the 70 level.

RSI TRADING SIGNALS

Because the RSI has been around for so long, traders have developed signals for trading-range markets and for trending markets. Some traders have run moving averages on the RSI to smooth out the readings, and other traders use trend lines and look for patterns. Certainly you are welcome to explore these approaches, but let's start with some simple signals for trading-range markets, because we are very likely to encounter that kind of situation.

If we start by using the 70 and 30 levels for the RSI as our trigger mechanism and we wait for the market to show us that it is turning up, then our signal to go long in a sideways market comes when the RSI falls below 30 and then climbs back above it. Naturally, long positions are entered on the day after the signal, so you are not catching the extreme low and are missing some of the profit potential of the signal. By waiting for the RSI to turn back up, you hope to eliminate the possibility of the market declining even further, and to avoid the purchase of something that is still falling. (Some traders anticipate the move back above 30 by a day or so, by buying when the RSI turns up from the oversold area under 30.) See Figures 15.1 and 15.2.

Figure 15.1: A 1-Year Daily Bar Chart with 14-Day RSI

DOW JONES 30   9771.85   0.000   0.000%
D: 01/30/01   O: 10702.19   H: 10900.77   L: 10682.96   C: 10881.20   Y: 11699.22

Prophet Financial Systems, Inc. (www.prophetfinance.com) Used by permission.

This example of the DJIA during 2001, as it trends slightly lower, illustrates several oversold buy and overbought sell signals that work fairly successfully. The small double bottom in March–April is a nice oversold signal, with the second low higher on the index. The big selloff in September shows that a market can always get more oversold; wait for the indicator to turn up.

Figure 15.2: A 1-Year Daily Bar Chart with 14-Day RSI

Prophet Financial Systems, Inc. (www.prophetfinance.com) Used by permission.

Here we have the S&P 500. Look at the small double bottom in March–April. Here we make a lower low on the index but the RSI makes a higher low. This is a good bullish divergence between the price action and the indicator. In the May–September downtrend, the RSI gets up near 60 only as the rallies fail.

Futures traders know that there is just as much profit potential and it is just as easy to go short as it is to go long. On the upside, the signal to go short is when the RSI rises above 70 and then declines back below it. See Figures 15.3 and 15.4.

THE FAILURE SWING

Another technique used by traders to generate buy and sell signals is to look for failure swings. Traders use this technique because it is a strong indication of a reversal. A failure swing is a basic trend reversal signal. For a top failure swing you must have a high over 70 on the RSI followed by a dip to a trough. The RSI needs to rise to a lower peak and then decline below the trough

Figure 15.3: A 1-Year Daily Bar Chart with 14-Day RSI

Agnico Eagle Mines 11.55 0.030 0.260%
D: 01/22/01 O: 6.19 H: 6.81 L: 6.12 C: 6.81 Y: 11.95

Prophet Financial Systems, Inc. (www.prophetfinance.com) Used by permission.

The stock begins a strong uptrend in April. The dips that you could buy show the 14-day RSI reaching only 40 before the stock rallies again. In an uptrending market, oversold buy signals need to be raised to 40. In October the stock has a correction and the oversold readings get to 30 and below.

Figure 15.4: A 5-Year Weekly Bar Chart with 14-Week RSI

Johnson & Johnson 59.70 -0.129 -0.216%
D: 02/03/97 O: 29.00 H: 29.94 L: 28.31 C: 29.87 Y: 60.47

Prophet Financial Systems, Inc. (www.prophetfinance.com) Used by permission.

RSI can be applied to weekly charts. The stock has been in a major uptrend for several years. Here we have an internal uptrend line; at the points where the trend line is tested, the RSI gets down to only 40. The stock slows a bit in 2000–2001, and the RSI reaches the 30 level for two major buys.

between the two peaks. A bottom failure swing needs a trough below the 30 level followed by a peak and then a higher trough. After the higher trough or low, the RSI must rise above the peak between the two troughs.

Another approach is to go long when you see a bullish divergence between the price action and the RSI; prices make the same low or a slightly lower low and the RSI makes a higher low, provided the first low or trough is below 30. Some traders feel that if the divergence makes a failure swing, it is a stronger signal to follow. See Figure 15.5.

Figure 15.5: A 3-Year Weekly Bar Chart with a 14-Week RSI

Prophet Financial Systems, Inc. (www.prophetfinance.com) Used by permission.

Market leader and Dow-Jones component IBM has been stuck in a broad sideways trend for three years. The 14-week RSI has generated three really good sells and three really good buys during this broad trading range. Notice how IBM went to a new low at the end of 2000 and the RSI did not make a lower low. This is the classic failure swing on the downside. (See Figure 15.7 for a failure swing on the upside.)

I'm not sure how you could test whether this observation holds up under scrutiny, but in general, the more signals or confirmation you get for a trade, the more successful it should be. The reverse signal, to go short, would be a bearish divergence whereby the first peak or high for the RSI is above 70. Of course, a failure swing in addition to the divergence would be favored.

The following table is a good way to remember how to apply the RSI in different circumstances.

TYPE OF MARKET	OVERBOUGHT	OVERSOLD
Trading Range	70	30
Uptrend	80	40
Downtrend	60	20

SIGNALS IN TRENDING MARKETS

Two trade entry rules are common in trending markets. Because we are dealing with a trending market and not a sideways market, your overbought and oversold levels should be adjusted and you should take signals only in the direction of the trend—follow only buy signals in an uptrend and sell signals in a downtrend.

ENTRY

Entry Rule One: In a clearly defined uptrend, go long or add to longs when the RSI falls below the oversold point (raised to 40 because of the uptrend) and climbs back above it. A failure swing should mean a stronger signal. See Figure 15.6.

Entry Rule Two: In a clearly defined downtrend, go short or add to shorts when the RSI rises above the overbought point (lowered to 60 because of the downtrend) and falls back below it. Again, a failure swing would mean you have a stronger signal. See Figure 15.7.

Figure 15.6: 3-Year Weekly Bar Chart with a 14-Week RSI

Hudson River Bancorp (Nasdaq NM) 23.21 -0.689 -2.88%
D: 01/25/99 O: 11.75 H: 11.94 L: 11.63 C: 11.63 Y: 27.22

Prophet Financial Systems, Inc. (www.prophetfinance.com) Used by permission.

This chart of HBRT shows two things to watch. First, in a strong uptrend like the one in 2000 and 2001, overbought signals need to be raised to 80. Second, as the stock climbs to a new high at the end of 2001 and into 2002, RSI makes a lower high to give us a bearish divergence and a sell signal going forward.

EXIT

Can the RSI be used for exit signals? Of course. Imagine you have an uptrend in place and you see a bearish divergence from the RSI. This divergence can be used to take profits on longs. Because we are in an uptrend and we may not have any confirmation from a trend-following indicator like an intermediate-term moving average, these highs will most often be temporary highs in the uptrend. The same thing can occur with downtrends. A bullish divergence from the RSI in a downtrend can be a good reason to cover shorts, but without a signal from a trend-following indicator, the lows are going to be temporary swing lows.

Figure 15.7: A 3-Year Weekly Bar Chart with a 14-Week RSI

Aol Time Warner Inc   29.58   -0.459   -1.52%
D: 02/08/99   O: 41.50   H: 41.70   L: 35.50   C: 39.63   Y: 104.48

Prophet Financial Systems, Inc. (www.prophetfinance.com) Used by permission.

AOL was in a strong downtrend during 2000 and early 2001. Notice how the rallies only managed to reach RSI readings of 60 throughout the downtrend. This is how the RSI needs to be adjusted in trending markets. The oversold readings of 30 in the time period did not produce very good rallies, either.

Earlier, we mentioned that some analysts draw trend lines and look for patterns in the RSI. A break of a trend line drawn on the RSI can indicate an important shift in the existing trend; but because the RSI is a secondary indicator, you must follow the price action.

Stochastics

If you thought wedges, triangles, and flags were strange names for investment approaches, try stochastics. What is a stochastic? According to the dictionary, *stochastic* comes from a Greek word meaning "to guess at." It is defined as denoting conjecture, involving a random variable, or involving probability or chance.

The stochastic oscillator, or stochastic for short, is a momentum oscillator, and a very popular technical tool whose use dates back to the 1950s (or the 1960s, depending on your source).

The stochastic oscillator seems to have been the creation of George C. Lane (but some people claim it was actually someone else's discovery). He has been working with and teaching this technical tool for several decades, and has become associated with it in nearly everyone's mind.

THE LOGIC OF STOCHASTICS

Supposedly, the stochastic oscillator, not unlike other indicators, developed from an observation about price action. The RSI by Wilder looked at the closing price relative to the previous closing prices, but the stochastic looks at where the close fell relative to the recent range. When the close moves away from either the high or the low, we know that the bulls or the bears are losing strength.

I remember George Lane speaking at one of the annual conferences of the Market Technicians Association, "When people are bullish, they buy and markets tend to close near their highs.

231

When people are bearish and they want to sell, you see the closes near the lows of the day."

Go ahead and look at any chart. Look at where the closes are at the tops of rallies. Look at where the closes are at bottoms. Do you doubt this observation? Go on-line or pick up a chart book. Examine any bar chart. What do you find at tops and bottoms? If you find this observation truthful from empirical observations, the next question is how to express it in a simple formula that converts what the eye sees subjectively into something more mathematical.

CALCULATING STOCHASTICS

Lane created a ratio by taking the close in relation to its low divided by the range for a particular time interval, and multiplying the result by 100. A percentage number is derived that is called %K. The user needs to define the number of time intervals (usually days) that the calculation will cover. This measure, %K, can be averaged to create %D. Lane recommends a 3-period smoothing of %K to generate the %D. The %K and the %D can be charted and graphed, with levels fluctuating from zero (0) to 100.

The %K and %D lines can be plotted along the bottom of a bar chart or candle chart, with zero at the bottom and 100 at the top. The upper part of the scale, in the 80 to 100 range, is considered overbought, and the range with the best sell signals is in the 85 to 90 area. The lower part, from 20 to 0, is considered oversold, and the range with the best buy signals occurs where the value of the %D is in the 10 to 15 area.

The formula for a basic stochastic indicator is:

$$\%K = \frac{Ct - Ln}{Hn - Ln} \times 100$$

where Ct = the closing price today
Ln = the lowest low for n days
Hn = the highest high for n days
N = the number of days (5 days is the usual default)
%D = %K smoothed over three days

Most charting packages use a solid line to display the %D and a dashed line for the smoothed %K, but be careful because some books and Web sites may have these percentages reversed. Sometimes, two different colored lines are used. We noted that 80 and 20 are the overbought and oversold levels to watch for, but some analysts suggest you watch for signals over 70 and below 30. See Figure 16.1.

What we have been describing is the basic or fast stochastic. Some analysts find this measure too sensitive, so they use a slow stochastic. How do we get the slow stochastic? First, the %D of the fast or basic stochastic, which has already been smoothed by

Figure 16.1: A 1-Year Daily Bar Chart with a 10-Day Fast Stochastic Indicator

Prophet Financial Systems, Inc. (www.prophetfinance.com) Used by permission.

IBM is shown here with a fast stochastic indicator along the bottom. Notice how quickly the fast indicator swings back and forth from the extremes as prices move. Both the solid and the dashed lines are percentages, and the better signals come from above 80 and below 20. Compare this to the signals from the slow stochastic in Figure 16.2.

Figure 16.2: A 1-Year Daily Bar Chart with a 10-Day Slow Stochastic Indicator

Intl Business Machines   114.25   -5.64   -4.70%
D: 01/23/01   O: 109.56   H: 109.94   L: 107.62   C: 109.06   Y: 125.40

Prophet Financial Systems, Inc. (www.prophetfinance.com) Used by permission.

IBM is shown in this example with a slow stochastic indicator along the bottom. Comparing this to the fast stochastic in Figure 16.1, we have fewer signals. The indicator still moves actively back and forth from the extremes as prices move. Notice the rally in October–December 2001. The price of the stock makes new highs for three months, but the stochastic makes lower highs. This is foreshadowing a price decline that starts to unfold in January 2002.

three periods, becomes the %K of the slow stochastic. The %D of the slow stochastic is %D of the fast stochastic smoothed again over another three periods. See Figure 16.2.

THE STOCHASTIC IN OPERATION

Like all indicators, these tools have good points and bad points. The stochastic oscillator is most effective in flat or broad trading-range markets, or in slow-moving trending markets. If you apply the stochastic oscillator to a typical or even a fast-moving trend, you should be careful to take only signals in the direction of the trend, and to look for confirmation from trend-following indicators like moving averages. Remember that a stochastic oscillator cannot be applied to the data taken from a close-only or line chart, or from a point-and-figure chart, because the stochastic needs to look at the range of prices as well as the close. See Figure 16.3.

Figure 16.3: A 1-Year Daily Bar Chart with a 10-Day Slow Stochastic Indicator

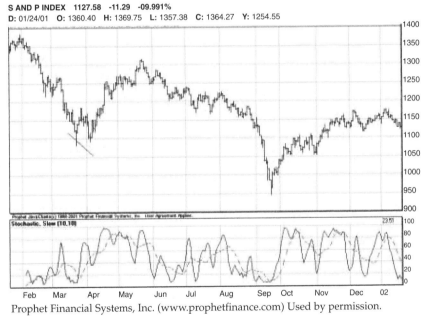

Prophet Financial Systems, Inc. (www.prophetfinance.com) Used by permission.

This chart shows the classic "go long" signal with a bullish divergence in the first trough of the %D below 30 during the middle of March. Prices make a lower low in early April, but the %D makes a higher low (the solid line). The S&P rallies 200 points from the signal, or better than 18%. This kind of return makes watching for these setups worthwhile. The index gets oversold in September, but without the bullish divergence.

SIGNALS

There are several trading rules and patterns for interpreting stochastic signals. The basic signals involve divergences and crossovers to generate trades in sideways markets. A signal to go long is a bullish divergence, whereby the price makes lower lows and the %D makes a higher low, especially when the first low is below 30. A signal to go short is a bearish divergence, whereby the first peak in the %D is above 70. Lane also identified another divergence pattern that needs three peaks. This triple divergence has a first peak followed by a lower second peak, but with a third peak in the %D that is higher than the second peak but lower than the first peak. Some reference books refer to this pattern as Lane's Classic Divergence Signal. See

Figure 16.4: A 1-Year Daily Bar Chart with a 10-Day Slow Stochastic Indicator

DOW JONES 30 9771.85 0.000 0.000%
D: 01/22/01 O: 10581.90 H: 10634.36 L: 10509.92 C: 10578.20 Y: 11194.29

Prophet Financial Systems, Inc. (www.prophetfinance.com) Used by permission.

Here we see an example of Lane's Classic Divergence Signal during April and May. The DJIA is making new highs for the move up, but notice the solid line or %D of the slow stochastic. The %D makes a peak in late April. The second peak of the %D in early May is lower than the first peak, but the third peak in late May is higher than the second peak and lower than the first peak.

Figure 16.4. (Lane has described at least six other patterns, such as left and right crossovers, hinges, warnings, extremes, setups, and failures. These patterns are more difficult to use and somewhat unreliable.)

For trending markets, the rules are modified a bit, but the changes should not be too much of a surprise. As noted earlier, signals from momentum indicators should be taken to enter in the direction of the trend or to get out of a position if a trend-following indicator has given a signal. The first entry rule in a trending market is to go long when either stochastic line (%K or %D) crosses below 30. A buy stop to go long is placed above the high of the signal day or any following day with a lower low. A protective sell stop is then placed below the low of the same day. See Figure 16.5.

Figure 16.5: A 9-Month Daily Bar Chart with a 10-Day Slow Stochastic Indicator

Prophet Financial Systems, Inc. (www.prophetfinance.com) Used by permission.

The rally in ASA Ltd during October–January shows how oversold readings (below 30) in the %D, the solid line, can be used to add to positions or enter positions within the direction of the trend. The combination of using a simple trend line and just one overbought or oversold indicator can be very helpful in identifying entry points.

On the upside, when either stochastic line (%K or %D) crosses over 70, a sell stop order to enter a new position is placed below the low of the signal day or any subsequent day with a higher high (i.e., the uptrend is maintained). A protective buy stop is then placed above the high of the same day. See Figure 16.6.

Figure 16.6: A 9-Month Daily Bar Chart with a 10-Day Slow Stochastic

Prophet Financial Systems, Inc. (www.prophetfinance.com) Used by permission.

If you combined a trend line with the stochastic indicator, you could have found two good opportunities to short or sell the popular Nasdaq 100 Trust (QQQs) on the way down to the September low. Using the move in the %D over 80 as the index approached or touched the trend line is an effective entry signal with trending markets.

Finally, trend-following indicators like moving averages can be used to take profits on positions in an established uptrend or downtrend when a crossing of the moving average confirms the shift in trend. If we don't get a crossover from a moving average or some other indicator, the overbought and oversold signals from the stochastic indicator are most likely going to point out only swing highs and lows and not trend reversals. See Figure 16.7.

Interpretation of signals can become pretty subjective. We have talked about signals above 70 and below 30, but you should be alert for signals in the 75 to 85 area on the upside and 15 to 25 area on the downside. No matter what levels you become comfortable with for signals, you should remember that when prices trend higher or are flat and the closes dip within the range, the market is internally weak, no matter what the numbers are.

The stochastic indicator can be applied to daily, weekly, and monthly charts. Short-term traders have applied them to intraday charts, and many traders find the signals to be effective. Many traders combine the stochastic indicator with the RSI,

Figure 16.7: A 5-Year Weekly Bar Chart with a 40-Week Moving Average and a 10-Week Slow Stochastic

GE-General Electric MA(40)

Prophet Financial Systems, Inc. (www.prophetfinance.com) Used by permission.

This chart shows that in 1999 and 2000, the overbought sell signals did not interrupt the strong uptrend of the stock and did not signal a reversal as it stayed above the 40-week or 200-day moving average. A reversal wasn't indicated until the prices fell below the long-term moving average.

placing the two indicators below the price chart. Some traders set the indicators to the same time frame; then they look for the two indicators to give similar setups. Other traders vary the time frames, hoping the shorter time frame indicator will give an early alert and the slow indicator will confirm the first signal.

A Few Logical Indicators to Follow

In Chapter 11, I mentioned that the time frame selected for the moving average should make some logical sense or relate to the market in some way. In Chapter 16, we learned that the stochastic oscillator came from an observation about price action and has a logical basis that you can understand. Other indicators should also make logical sense.

In this chapter, we discuss several other indicators that make logical sense and are worth the time involved in tracking them: the advance/decline line (A/D line) and some of its variations, the Arms Index, the last-hour indicator, a few sentiment indicators, and the Barron's Confidence Index (which is a hybrid, dealing with both logic and sentiment). There are many more indicators, but this short list will give you a good foundation for market timing in stocks and bonds.

THE ADVANCE/DECLINE LINE

The advance/decline line dates back to the late 1920s and 1930s and was developed by Colonel Leonard P. Ayers. Ayers headed a firm called Standard Statistics which was eventually merged into a firm by the name of Poor's. (Yes, it is the well-recognized Standard & Poor's, a division of McGraw-Hill.) He tracked a lot of data to survey business conditions and the sentiment among businesspeople—whether they had confidence to invest in new plants and equipment. In addition, Ayers followed the number of stocks that rose and the number that fell each day on the stock exchange. This foreshadowed what we know today as the advance/decline line (A/D line). The basic tracking of the A/D line, its compilation and interpretation, is not hard to understand, and it makes logical sense.

CALCULATING THE A/D LINE

Every trading day, individual stocks can do one of three things: They can rise, they can fall, or they can remain unchanged. Most calculations of the A/D line ignore the number of unchanged stocks, leaving us to follow the difference between the advancing issues and the declining issues. Through numbers, the A/D line looks at the breadth and confidence of a market movement. The A/D line is a cumulative market breadth indicator and is generally used in comparison to a market index like the DJIA. The level of the A/D line is not important, but its trend is. Besides subtracting the declining issues from the advancing issues, some analysts divide the number of advancers by the number of decliners. Other analysts look at the absolute value of the number of advancing issues minus the number of declining issues; this is called absolute breadth.

HOW THE A/D LINE WORKS

It is understandable that at a market bottom, investors tend to buy the better-known companies, but as a stock market advance continues and the economy improves, more companies participate in the rally, the advance broadens out, and the A/D line rises. The more stocks that participate in an advance, the stronger it is; while the lower the number of stocks moving up in an advance, the greater the probability of a reversal. A strong market has many more advances than declines. This will continue, confirming the advance, but at some point the A/D line will peak before the final price high. The A/D line is a leading indicator, but why?

The A/D line peaks before the major averages for several reasons. First of all, we already know that the market is a discounting mechanism; it anticipates the business cycle. Stocks will peak and turn down before earnings turn down and before the general economy turns down. Besides the general movement of the stock market turning down before the economic numbers reverse, certain sectors of the economy are more sensitive, such as construction and consumer spending. Construction has a long lead time and is sensitive to the economy and to the direction of interest rates, making it one of the industries in which cutbacks can show up early. Consumer spending is dependent on discretionary income, and will weaken before spending slows on so-called essentials. As stocks in these two sectors turn down, they drag down the A/D line, causing the line to peak before the final price high in the average.

Another important factor is that approximately 40% of the securities on the New York Stock Exchange are interest-rate-sensitive. This includes banks, brokerage companies, insurance companies, utilities, and preferred stocks, among others. The profitability of banks and savings and loans is influenced by their net interest margin—the difference between what they have to pay for money and what they can receive on their investments. Because these financial institutions normally borrow short and lend long, they do better in a falling-rate environment. Borrowing short means they offer an interest rate to depositors for a period of from 90 days to perhaps two or three years. Lending long means that they make loans that extend for perhaps 30 years. Long-term interest rates are normally higher than short-term rates, because of the uncertainty about inflation and risk associated with being paid back in the future with dollars that could be worth less. Banks pay a lower rate to get money from depositors in the short term. The banks then turn around and lend the money to borrowers at a higher rate. As interest rates fall, banks can reduce what they pay to depositors every 90 days, for example, while the rate they receive from borrowers stays locked in for several years.

In a falling-rate environment, a bank's net interest margin improves. The opposite happens in a rising-rate environment, because the money paid to depositors can go up faster than the average rate of the loan portfolio. Other things can affect the profitability of banks and thrifts, but you can see how interest rates affect them. The investment portfolios of insurance companies can rise and fall with rates, and brokerage houses make more money on margin accounts as rates rise. Utilities borrow extensively to build their plants, so the direction of interest rates can affect them significantly. This is why we consider stocks in these sectors to be interest-rate-sensitive.

Several studies have shown that interest rates start to rise approximately nine months before stock prices peak and turn lower. With interest rates leading stock prices by about nine months, it is no surprise that stocks that are sensitive to rising interest rates will also turn down before other stocks. The decline in interest-rate-sensitive stocks ahead of the general market also weakens the A/D line.

The last stocks to be sold in a mature bull market are the quality names that were first bought at the bottom. People sell interest-rate-sensitive stocks and speculative issues and everything else, but they hold those blue-chip, quality names. Because these stocks are the last to be sold, when they are dumped it is a sign of capitulation and can be a bottom signal to be alert for.

CONSTRUCTING THE A/D LINE

A/D lines can be started at any time and can be constructed for stocks, corporate bonds, industries, sectors, and even commodities. If you started an A/D line at zero (0), a string of down days can quickly turn the A/D line negative. Because of this, technicians usually start from some high, arbitrary number like 100,000, to keep the number series positive. This is shown in Table 17.1.

Table 17.1: The Advance/Decline Line

DAY	# OF ADVANCING ISSUES	# OF DECLINING ISSUES	DIFFERENCE	VALUE OF A/D LINE
1	1,800	1,400	+400	100,400
2	1,550	1,650	−100	100,300
3	1,780	1,490	+290	100,590
4	1,875	1,430	+445	101,035
5	1,575	1,645	−70	100,965
6	1,200	1,800	−600	100,365

In the table, we started with a large base number of 100,000. As we go from day one through day six, we compute the difference between the number of advancing issues and the number of declining issues, and add or subtract the result from the running total.

Because the number of issues listed on the New York Stock Exchange and other marketplaces keeps expanding, a simple A/D line gives greater weighting to more recent years with more issues rising and falling. To adjust for this, analysts who want to make comparisons going back several stock market cycles typically use a formula for the A/D line that takes the square root of the advancing stocks divided by the unchanged stocks, less the declining stocks divided by the unchanged stocks. This allows for a proper comparison over long periods of time. By giving some weight to the unchanged issues in the formula, it is easier to notice a slowdown in the momentum of the A/D line at an earlier point in time.

SIGNALS

If the market and the A/D line are moving up together, the rally is sound; but if you spot a negative divergence, with the averages rising while the A/D line is declining, then there is likely to be trouble ahead. Some technicians explain that the A/D line leads stock market turns in another way. As confidence weakens, money will move out of speculative and secondary stocks and into the better-quality blue-chip names.

Using the A/D line is tricky in that it tends to peak anywhere from five to ten months before the peak in the blue chips. While this is a long lead time to deal with, remember that once the A/D line stops rising, you should wonder how much longer the bull market will last. See Figures 17.1 and 17.2.

At a market bottom, the A/D line performs differently and does not lead the market. Usually, the DJIA will make its final price low, but the A/D line will keep falling as other sectors continue to be knocked lower. The better price action of the Dow compared to the new lows in the A/D line gives us a positive or

Figure 17.1: A 6-Month Daily Bar Chart with an Oscillator of
Advances and Declines

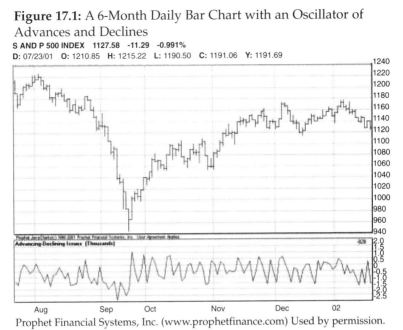

In September, the stock market rebounded sharply and the number of
advancing issues less the number of declining issues climbed as well.
In December, the stock market flattened out and the A/D numbers
started to slip.

Figure 17.2: A 6-Month Daily Bar Chart with an Oscillator of
Advances and Declines

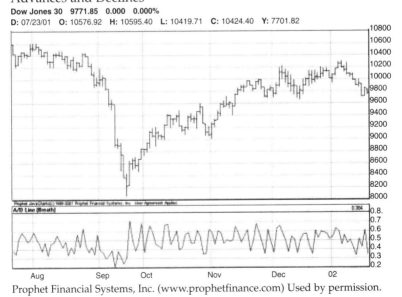

Here we have the DJIA with the advanced–decline ratio. The ratio of
advance issues to declining issues still rises sharply in September as
stocks rebound.

bullish divergence. The longer this divergence lasts, the more significant the ultimate reversal.

The A/D line signals can be grouped according to bearish and bullish interpretations. If the stock index is rising and the A/D line is falling, this is bearish. If the index is at or near a previous high or top while the A/D line is significantly below its corresponding top, this is bearish. Also, if the stock index is at or near a prior bottom but the A/D line is below its prior low, this should be interpreted as bearish in that the broad market list is still weak.

For the bulls, if the stock index is declining but the A/D line is rising, then the interpretation is bullish. If the index is at or near a prior top and the A/D line is significantly above its corresponding top, then this is bullish in that the broad market is attracting strong buying. If an index is at or near a previous bottom and the A/D line is above its low, then the divergence is positive.

THE LAST-HOUR INDICATOR

Another market-timing tool that is logical in its approach and easy to construct and maintain is the last-hour indicator. A technical analyst by the name of Stan Weinstein introduced this indicator in 1979. The last-hour indicator is constructed by cumulating the net point change in the DJIA between 3 P.M. EST and the 4 P.M. closing bell of the New York Stock Exchange. This cumulative net change line is then plotted on a chart of the DJIA. Usually, these two series move together, but there are times when divergences occur and they can be good leading indicators. An example is shown in Table 17.2.

Table 17.2: Last-Hour Indicator

DAY	DJIA AT 3 P.M.	DJIA at 4 P.M.	Net Change	Cumulative
1	10,350	10,370	+20	+20
2	10,480	10,495	+15	+35
3	10,590	10,650	+60	+95

How the Last-Hour Indicator Works

Stan Weinstein argued, and I believe correctly, that the last hour of trading represented the best indication of traders' and specialists' intentions. Traders know that the public usually reacts early in the day to company or economic news, and there can be various crosscurrents, so that getting a reading of the tape or a good sense of the market's direction can be difficult. Specialists try to make their money during the day, and they tend to balance their books for the next day late in the session. This leaves traders who are willing to hold positions overnight or who want to reduce positions as the dominant players at the end of the day. Traders who are bullish will buy or add to longs late in the day, and if they are uncertain or bearish they will also move before the close. The DJIA can close up on the day, but we may see traders reduce their positions in the last hour, demonstrating their growing uneasiness to hold long positions.

Signals

If we see a pattern in which the Dow continues to rise but it keeps losing points in the last hour of trading, it is an early warning signal for the Dow. Like the A/D line, a peak in the last-hour indicator often precedes a downturn in stock prices. When looking for bottoms, the reverse will operate. The DJIA can make new lows, but what will forecast an eventual reversal is if stocks improve in the last hour, creating a divergence between the last-hour indicator and the Dow. As with other technical indicators, the longer this divergence goes on, the more powerful the reversal.

The Last-Half-Hour Indicator

In 1985, I adapted the last-hour indicator to the Treasury bond futures market by cumulating the net change in 32nds in the last 30 minutes of trading of the T-bond future at the Chicago Board of Trade. By testing 60-minute and 15-minute periods, I found that locals and day traders would square their positions in the last half-hour of trading. This left just the action of traders who really wanted to hold longs overnight or wanted to reduce their positions because they were worried about a decline. Tracking the last half-hour of trading in futures and plotting it against the T-bond contract produces a leading indicator that doesn't require a lot of work.

THE ARMS INDEX

The Arms Index or the short-term trading index is another indicator worth maintaining and tracking. The Arms Index might be the most recognized overbought or oversold indicator among stock traders. Richard W. Arms Jr. created this index, which is also known as the trading index, or TRIN or MKDS on quote machines.

CONSTRUCTING THE ARMS INDEX

The Arms Index (TRIN) is derived by dividing the ratio of the number of advancing issues to the number of declining issues, by the ratio of the volume of advancing issues to the volume of declining issues. Daily New York Stock Exchange data is used in the calculation.

$$\frac{\text{Number of Advancing Issues / Number of Declining Issues}}{\text{Volume of Advancing Issues / Volume of Declining Issues}}$$

TRIN compares the volume needed to advance a stock to the amount required to produce a declining issue. A bullish condition in the stock market is indicated when less volume is needed to generate an advancing stock than a declining stock. This usually happens when stocks are oversold. A bearish condition is found when heavy volume is needed to advance an issue and relatively less volume is needed to produce a decline. The Arms Index measures the relative strength of advancing volume compared to declining volume. If more volume goes into advancing stocks than declining stocks, the index will be less than 1.00. If more volume is seen in declining stocks than advancing stocks, then the index will be over 1.00. See Figure 17.3.

Figure 17.3: A 1-Year Daily Bar Chart with the ARMS Index

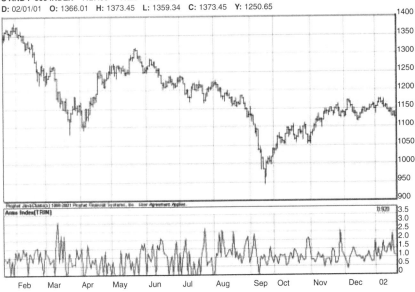

S AND P 500 INDEX   1127.58   -11.29   -0.991%
D: 02/01/01   O: 1366.01   H: 1373.45   L: 1359.34   C: 1373.45   Y: 1250.65

Prophet Financial Systems, Inc. (www.prophetfinance.com) Used by permission.

The ARMS Index or TRIN compared to the S&P 500. Notice the low readings during April–July, and the stronger readings in October–December.

MODIFYING THE ARMS INDEX

Over the years, traders and analysts have tried many ways to look at and smooth TRIN readings. Some people take a 10-day or 30-day open trading index. This approach uses a 10-day total of each of the four inputs to construct the ratio. Other people find that 40 days is a better time frame for them, and they average the 4 P.M. TRIN readings. The higher this averaged or smoothed TRIN reading, the more oversold the market; the lower the reading, the more overbought.

Extreme oversold readings are one way of recognizing a high-volume selling climax and a potential market bottom with this indicator. Naturally, some analysts have constructed a TRIN for the Nasdaq and the AMEX.

SENTIMENT

Sentiment is an important part of the investment scene, and if it can be measured and followed, then it is another valuable tool to help you make investment decisions. I divide sentiment into three categories: what analysts and traders are saying, what traders are doing, and anecdotal information. Let's take a look at these in turn.

WHAT'S BEING SAID

A number of investor surveys try to formally measure what investment professionals are recommending—that is, what they are saying. *Investors Intelligence* takes a weekly survey of investment advisors to see how many are bullish, how many are bearish, and how many are expecting a correction in the stock market. The *Bullish Consensus*® survey by the Market Vane Corporation polls various commodity players. The reasoning is that if people follow the advice of professionals and take a position in the market, then the market becomes overbought when too many people have bullish recommendations. When everyone recommends that you go long, and you act, who is left to buy? On the downside, when no one is recommending the market, it is probably oversold and due for a rally.

Survey results are typically expressed as a percentage, and the numbers can go from 0 (zero) to 100. Because Wall Street, LaSalle Street, and Main Street all like the long side of the market for a variety of reasons, the midpoint of these surveys should actually be higher than 50 to compensate for the bias to be long. Several of these surveys can be found in *Barron's* each week. In fact, *Barron's* conducts several investor surveys and roundtables where you can get a sense of the tone of the market and how committed the professionals are to the market.

A few specialized surveys exist for the fixed-income markets. Here professionals are monitored for their recommendations and actions respective to their benchmarks. Fixed-income bond funds are structured by their maturity, the products they invest in, and credit risk. In a normal, positive yield curve environment, the longer the maturity, the higher the yield, and the shorter the maturity, the lower the yield. When fixed-income managers are saying they are long their benchmarks, they are bullish; if they are short their benchmarks, they are bearish. Fund managers invest within the guidelines of each fund. As an example, one fund might be established to invest in Treasuries of up to five years in maturity. Portfolio managers who think rates could decline in the months ahead usually want to extend the average maturity of their portfolios to lock in today's interest rate for as long as possible (going long their benchmark). If rates are set to rise, managers usually shorten maturities (go short their benchmark), so when issues mature they can be rolled over (reinvested) at the new higher rates that are prevailing. Surveys of fixed-income portfolio managers report only what these managers decide to share, which may or may not be their actual positions.

What People Are Doing

The next category of sentiment is what people are actually doing. Here we are trying to measure what people are doing and not saying. We look at transactions and not words. Tools exist for both the fixed-income markets and equities.

Short-Term Interest Rates

Money market funds represent the short end of the yield curve. There is a quick and easy way to find out what money market fund managers are doing. These managers invest in relatively short-term instruments, typically with maturities of less than one year in length. Today, there are hundreds of money market funds with trillions of dollars under management. When these fund managers extend or lengthen maturities, they expect rates to decline; when they shorten maturities, they are anticipating rising rates ahead. How do we know what they are doing? Simply look in the credit market report in the *Wall Street Journal* or the *New York Times* on Thursdays. The number to follow is the average maturity of securities held in portfolios of taxable money market funds. Historically, a maturity of around 29 days is short and a maturity of 65 days is on the long side.

To see what money managers are doing in the long end of the interest rate curve, look at the direction of some of the yield spreads. The logic is easy to follow. If you manage fixed-income money and can move it around on the yield curve, you will lengthen or shorten maturities. If you expect rates to decline, you lengthen, and if you expect rates to rise, you get defensive and shorten. Checking the movement of prices or rates on the 10-year note and the 30-year bond is just one way of seeing what professionals are doing with the money.

PUT/CALL RATIOS

Another method of watching what traders are doing is to analyze option transactions. As long as greed and fear remain basic human emotions, traders will give us important clues through their option transactions. The put/call ratio is a sentiment indicator and is interpreted in a contrary fashion. When a market heats up and has been in a strong rise, speculative activity increases in the call option market. The public tends to buy too many calls at a market top. This is greed at work. A call option represents the right to go long on a stock, commodity, or bond at a given price, or what is known as the strike price. A premium in dollars is paid for the right to go long. Instead of looking to buy stocks and hold them for 18 months, the option buyer expects to turn a profit in three months or less. Three months is not a very long time to be proven right. If the price of the security does not climb above the strike price, the option has no value. A small amount of money can control a large option position, and this is where greed comes in. As a market rise continues, more people become convinced it will go on forever, with traders reaching for calls, betting on the rise to never falter.

When the volume of call options traded is heavy relative to the number of puts traded, it is a sign that the market is overbought. The reverse happens when the market has been in a decline. At a market bottom, the public will be bearish and will buy puts more actively, while call volume will be light. The movement in the put/call ratio is very interesting and has proven to be a good indicator.

Using a contrary approach, low readings in the put/call ratio are bearish and high readings are bullish. Most people smooth the numbers out by a 5- or 10-day moving average. Because this is a ratio, you need to see if the ratio becomes lopsided when either or both of the numbers are low. If you are using put/call ratios as a signal, the figures should have heavy volume as well as being lopsided.

FUN WITH SENTIMENT

The last sentiment approach is anecdotal. Here we are talking about the famous shoeshine boy story and the magazine cover. Anecdotal stories are subjective and only good when you are not looking for them. Traditionally, the thinking goes that when someone who is far removed from Wall Street becomes interested in stocks, the rally has gone on for too long. That was the case of the shoeshine boy asking John D. Rockefeller for a stock tip in 1929. Or perhaps it was an Aunt in Peoria, Illinois, or a brother in Topeka, Kansas, who called out of the blue in the early part of the summer of 1987 to ask about the stock market and what's good to buy. These are signals that the rally is very mature.

Technical analyst Paul Montgomery has researched the cover of *Time* magazine. Looking back at cover stories for 60 years, Montgomery found that when an economic, stock market, or financial cover graced a general news magazine like *Time*, the trend was nearly over. The trend might continue for another three or four months, but Montgomery calculated that 12 months later, the highlighted financial market had moved in the opposite direction 85% of the time. This is a simple approach, but a pretty powerful indicator all the same.

Anecdotal signals do not give you a strong cause-and-effect indicator, but they alert you to the idea that the prevailing trend has gone on too long, and nearly everyone knows about it or has taken advantage of it. From that point forward, look for a reversal pattern or some other real signal that the trend has changed.

THE BARRON'S CONFIDENCE INDEX

The Barron's Confidence Index is one of the oldest sentiment indicators, dating back to 1932. It is a hybrid indicator of sorts in that it is included under sentiment but it also has strong logical support. The Confidence Index, or BCI for short, can be found each week in *Barron's*. It is calculated (on Thursdays) by dividing the average yield of high-grade corporate bonds by the average yield of intermediate-grade speculative bonds. The resulting number can be found in the Market Laboratory section of *Barron's* under bonds. An example is shown in Table 17.3.

Table 17.3

	LAST WEEK	PREV. WEEK	YR. AGO WEEK
Best-Grade Bonds	6.65	6.65	6.87
Intermediate-Grade Bonds	7.79	7.74	7.72
Confidence Index	85.4	85.9	89.0

THE LOGIC OF BCI

The logic behind this indicator is this: Investors with foresight move into the best- or better-grade bonds when they anticipate economic weakness or a recession ahead. A bond is an obligation to pay interest (and ultimately the principal) that can extend for many years, so when investors sense that the economy may weaken, they want to be in the best or strongest companies. Odds are that the companies in the best financial strength will be the ones that can weather a slowdown. At this point in the business cycle, investors lack confidence in the economy and bid up the price of the higher-quality bonds, which makes their yield decline (bond yields move inversely with price), and the BCI decreases.

At the bottom of a recession, when the worst is behind us and astute investors see a recovery ahead and have more confidence, investors shift money into more risky bonds. These lower-quality bonds are selling at perhaps 80 or 70 cents on the dollar; their yield has been pushed up to compensate investors for what the marketplace believes is more risk. As money flows into these bonds, their prices rise and their yields decline, and in turn the BCI rises.

SIGNALS

In an article published in *Barron's* in 1959, Joe Granville showed how he was using the BCI as a stock market timing tool. If investors gained more confidence to buy riskier bonds, then they would also invest in stocks. Granville found that the BCI led stock prices at turning points by two to four months. In the late 1980s, I applied the BCI to the Treasury bond futures market and found that it was a coincident leading indicator for bonds. Low readings in the BCI signaled tops in bonds, and high readings gave a buy signal. Because shifts in interest rates precede turns in stocks, the BCI is important to follow. The best part of following it is that it is so simple. All you have to do is buy *Barron's* every Saturday, or check it on-line and look in the Laboratory Section for the latest figures.

A FINAL WORD

Sentiment indicators should be part of your toolbox. Remember that they typically lead and should be used as a wake-up call to potential reversals. You will hear many anecdotal stories; pay attention only to extremes.

Overcoming the Pitfalls: Real-World Technical Analysis

No investment approach is perfect. There are pitfalls to using any approach, and technical analysis is no exception. In using technical analysis, some of the problems stem from not understanding the construction and limitations of the various indicators—the leads, lags, and faults. However, more problems come from human error and from expecting too much from these tools.

The fact that some of these tools are based on mathematical formulas does not increase or guarantee their success. We have already noted that some tools, such as oscillators, work better in some environments than others. In addition, over time some indicators have stopped working because of structural changes in the markets, so you need to develop new twists and new indicators as you go along. You need to understand the current environment to temper buy and sell signals in a bear market or a bull market, and you need to look for better setups to trade as well as to test.

Other problems come from the subjective nature of chart reading. Pattern recognition is a skill that needs to be developed with day-to-day practice and, in the end, not everyone acquires the knack of it. Even if you become good at reading charts, you can still get hurt by false breakouts and failed patterns. The chart examples selected for this book all work, but that is not the real world. In the real world, you can encounter whipsaws. Whipsaws are repeated, sharp trend reversals that cause most trend-following and breakout systems to give you a string of losses. We have discussed how to use filters (see Chapter 4) and

2-moving-averages systems to cut down on whipsaws (see Chapter 11), but nothing is foolproof. Losses will occur, but the key to success is in how you deal with them.

DEALING WITH CHANGE

Everything you own is changing in price and value. Some things change slowly in value, like your house, condo, raw land, or antiques; and some change rapidly, like that Internet stock you bought in 1999. Your basic objective when it comes to investing is to profit from change. The art of investing is to recognize change and adjust to it. Neither you nor I will overcome all of the obstacles (the markets never make it easy, and without risk the reward would be much smaller), but if you develop a disciplined yet dynamic approach, you will be miles ahead of the person with no plan whatsoever. The pitfalls will always change, so even if we suggest how to overcome some of them, more will spring up. The best way to deal with them is to have an approach that provides for self-analysis.

SIX INVESTMENT GUIDELINES TO FOLLOW

Because life and investments are always changing and no investment approach is perfect, I recommend six rules to guide you through the pitfalls of investing—or at least to give you some help with them. Investing is a lifetime skill; work at it now and use these guidelines for years to come.

1. WRITE THINGS DOWN

By writing things down you will be able to review and analyze your good investments and your bad ones. If you cannot examine what made you pick an investment, then you are probably doomed to repeat your mistakes. Investing is a skill, and skills are learned by successful repetition. To repeat successes in the investment arena, you need to know what you did right and hone those skills.

2. KEEP A CHECKLIST OR DIARY

To best understand yourself and your abilities, maintain a checklist for every trade or investment. At a minimum, answer the following basic questions:

- How much money are you committing?
- What is your profit or price objective?
- What are you willing to risk? [Express it in points or dollars.]
- How long do you expect to be in the trade or investment?

3. HAVE ONE SINGLE REASON FOR YOUR ACTION

This may sound strange, but instead of finding a laundry list of reasons for your purchase, try to find the one key reason that made you buy or sell. It might have been a breakout from a large base formation, a close above a trend line, or crossing the 200-day moving average.

If a trade doesn't work out and you had multiple reasons for the purchase, it becomes extremely difficult to analyze the results and attempt to make corrections. Think about a trader on the floor of one of the commodity exchanges, the New York Stock Exchange, or the American Stock Exchange. These traders watch the tape or the action in the pit and they think on their feet: Buy, sell, or stand aside. If a stock makes a new high on the day, you go long. When you boil it down, short-term trading is basically simple, so try to keep it that way. If you find several good reasons for liking the security, then find the most compelling one, or the one that can stand on its own.

4. REVIEW YOUR CHARTS

Checking on the high, low, and close on a quote machine or over the Internet is not the same as actually looking at the chart with the latest price action. Review your charts every day. Keep a visual track of the instrument and then step back to see it on a chart. Think about a stock that closes slightly lower on the day.

By looking only at the price quote and not seeing that it closed on the low after a wide range, you could miss seeing a significant reversal to the downside. Likewise, a narrow range day may mean nothing until you see it at the end of a strong move up; then you see the trend failing.

Ideally, consider drawing your charts by hand or at least updating by hand the computer-drawn charts of the stocks in which you have positions. This point is especially important for novice traders. Keeping charts up by hand will force you to learn and to concentrate your focus on a short list of securities. By following just a small list of securities, you won't be overwhelmed or spread too thin. You don't have to follow everything, and you can drop dull stocks for ones that look more interesting. The stocks you focus on should change through the business cycle; for example, early in the cycle the financials do well, and late in the cycle energy stocks pick up.

5. REVIEW YOUR LONG-TERM CHARTS AND INDICATORS

Look at the longer-term charts and indicators every two weeks or more often. To do this, go to a Web site or subscribe to a commercial-chart book service. For example, if you went long on a signal from a daily chart and the stock has risen nicely, you need to check the longer-term charts to see if this security can become a longer-term position. This is also a very good way to look for investment ideas. By looking at weekly and monthly charts, you will find stocks with big bases, big tops, and good consolidation patterns. Write down the symbol and the name of that stock with the 4-month base pattern, and then drill down to a daily chart. The pattern should look just as interesting on a daily chart. This is how you can be a buyer at or near the breakout point. This is how you will find your own investment ideas. Finding and acting on your own ideas is not only tremendously satisfying, but in addition, your selections may be ahead of the Wall Street crowd. They may not add a stock to the recommended list until it has already been marked up significantly. The same goes for the indicators we discussed in Chapter 17. Check the Barron's Confidence Index for extreme readings;

check the direction of the advance/decline line. What are the sentiment indicators showing? If your indicators are diverging, then you want to be more selective.

6. KEEP A CHART PATTERNS BOOK

Record any chart pattern that looks interesting in a special book. By looking back at chart patterns to see how they turn out, you will improve your skills. This will help you become better able to pick out good-looking chart patterns in real time and not with hindsight. Your book might become your "would have, could have, should have" book, and you might find some fantastic winners in it, especially in a strong bull market. But don't kick yourself because you didn't buy or sell something. You can congratulate yourself that you are becoming a good stock picker and chart reader. Don't worry about any of the investments you didn't make; there will always be new ones, tomorrow or next week or in the next cycle. If you improve your skills at becoming a stock picker, you will always be able to find investments in the future.

EIGHT GUIDELINES FOR SUCCESSFUL TRADING

There are scores of self-help ideas for successful trading. For me, these eight are the most important. The list is short because the simple approach is often the best.

1. WAIT

This is a 4-letter word you can say in public. There are always new ideas and new investments and changing charts and stories. Never be in a rush to commit your hard-earned money to the market. Have patience. Find the right opportunity and the right setup. Wait until you find a stock just coming out of a 4-month base with increasing volume, rising moving averages, and superior relative strength. There are thousands of securities out there; wait for the best-looking ones.

2. CONFIRM

Earlier I suggested you find one simple reason for your decision to buy or sell. I stand by that advice, but I also suggest you seek confirmation of the pattern or signal. Does the volume confirm it? What about other techniques for confirming the price action?

3. DON'T EXPECT TOO MUCH

Treat each trade as just a trade. Don't talk yourself into finding the next stock that will climb tenfold and allow you to retire. This kind of thinking is not productive and can create two problems.

First, you are probably dealing with unreadable price targets, so your risk/reward ratio is unnaturally bullish. The risk is real, but the reward is inflated. Your risk is that price level or point where you will get out. This can be a close below a trend line or moving average, or the bottom of a price pattern. The reward should be a readable price objective from a formation, the return line of a channel, the upper band of a moving average envelope, or a level on a point-and-figure chart. Generally, look for opportunities to risk one dollar to make three. The three-to-one relationship will help tilt the odds in your favor.

The second problem that arises from high expectations is that when you buy a stock or bond and are looking for a home run, your judgment is altered. Think about this scenario: You buy a stock and you think it can go to the moon. The stock breaks a very short-term uptrend one day. Do you get out of the position, or do you rationalize staying in because the stock is ultimately going to do phenomenally well? What is the problem with a little break of a short-term uptrend line? The problem is discipline, and you just lost it. No matter how excited you are about the prospects for your investment, always treat it objectively. Many top traders think defensively first. The first question they ask themselves is: "Where can I get out if I'm wrong?" Cutting your losses is the only way to stay in the game.

4. Don't Trade Without Stops

"Trade with stops? Oh, I use mental stops." I have heard that comment too many times. I have never met anyone who was able to be a successful short-term trader by using "mental stops." A mental stop is just in your head. You may have written it down somewhere and you may have discussed it with your broker, but unless it is actually entered as an open order, it does you absolutely no good. If the stock goes through your mental stop order and then you see the stock come back, you have just reinforced something that can cost you dearly. This is not among the habits of a winner. Somewhere down the road the absence of a stop will give you that large loss you want to avoid. Look at Table 18.1. It shows, in no uncertain terms, that the more of your trading capital that is lost, the more remote the chance is that you will recover back to your starting level or turn a profit on your capital.

Table 18.1

PERCENTAGE LOSS	PERCENTAGE GAIN NEEDED ON REMAINING CAPITAL TO RECOVER
10%	11.1%
20%	25%
30%	42.8%
40%	66.7%
50%	100%
60%	150%

You now realize that you need to use stops, but where do you place them? Go back to the various patterns and signals and ask yourself, "Where am I wrong?" Where would a reversal happen? Where is support broken or resistance penetrated? Where does the trend line intersect? Where does the moving average intersect now? All of these are legitimate places for a stop loss order, in that the price action is telling you that your original observation and conclusion were wrong. There is nothing wrong with being wrong in a small way, but there is something wrong with being wrong in a big way. Remember, you want to avoid the big loss.

5. KEEP IT SIMPLE

When boiled down to its essence, trading is just buying, selling, or doing nothing. That's simple, right? Keep it that way, but have some structured decision-making rules—rules for trading, for entry, and for exit. A simple decision-making rule for entry could be trading at least one week above the x-period moving average or two closes above the x-week moving average.

6. WATCH FOR THE UNEXPECTED

Things happen, both good and bad; take advantage of them when they happen. A great pattern can go bad, as a result of political problems, global shortages, or whatever. If you are short into a bearish event, then cover. This may be an exaggerated move down, so grab it. On the upside, if an extra boost occurs because of an exogenous event, this move should be considered for profit-taking. If a random event happens and it goes against your position, get out as fast and as best you can. Stand aside and reappraise the situation without a position. If the reason you bought is still valid, you can always reenter.

7. DON'T FOLLOW TOO MANY INDICATORS

This rule goes along with the idea of keeping it simple. If you have a stable of indicators, you need to vary the time frames; otherwise, you get similar readings.

8. DON'T COUNT ON HOPE TO BAIL YOU OUT

Hope will not help you with a losing position. Cheerleading may make you feel good, but aside from that, the market doesn't care. Noticing greed and fear can make you money, but hope has no redeeming value in trading. Follow the price action; that is real. Hope is an illusion in the markets. Don't give it one more day; don't wait to get out. The risk is that it will only get worse. If it rallies back, you can always get in again, but you cannot make back losses through hope. On the other side, don't hope for some price level to be reached. Keep your objectivity with gains as well as losses.

Putting It All Together:
Case Studies

We know that virtually anything is easier to analyze with the benefit of 20/20 hindsight; chart analysis is no different. Unfortunately, we must learn to make decisions in real time and with real results. In today's rapidly changing financial environment, a trader or investor with a knowledge of charting and technical analysis is far better equipped than someone without any understanding of the nature of price movements.

IDENTIFY YOUR PERSONAL PROFILE

The biggest part of "putting it all together" is to come up with a personal plan. There are countless approaches to the markets, and *you* must decide on the plan that is best suited to you. Only you can assess your temperament, your abilities, your tolerance for losses, and your patience with winners. Once you make some personal decisions, you can build an approach that is in tune with your abilities, rather than trying to mold yourself to an unachievable ideal.

I have written this book as an analyst, but I suspect that most of you will probably be reading this book as a way to become a trader or to improve your investing. The roles of the analyst and trader are very different, and most people do not appreciate the particular skills involved in successful trading. A trader may start with some sort of analysis, but what really separates him or her from the analysts are money management and a unique psychology. An old Wall Street saying goes to the heart of the difference: "Forecasting sows the seed; trading reaps the harvest."

265

WILL YOU BE A TRADER OR AN ANALYST?

Traders should have a well-thought-out, written plan or, in the case of a floor trader, a plan that is so ingrained in the memory it is like second nature. A complete trading plan should include analysis or some way to select trades, money management, and a trading strategy that includes trade entry and exit. An analyst spends time looking at every recommendation from a dozen different angles, using three dozen different indicators. The successful trader also does some analysis, but it is kept very simple. The analyst strives to be correct with every recommendation, and is a level-money bettor (the same amount is bet on each trade), while the trader just wants to be more right than wrong on a series of trades. Proper money management is the single most important tool that separates the analyst from the trader, as well as separating the successful trader from the loser. Successful traders bet more heavily when they are right, and cut back positions quickly when they are wrong.

WHY MONEY MANAGEMENT IS CRITICAL

The main reason money management is crucial to successful trading and investing is that technical analysis is not a science. It is not black or white; there are no certainties, only probabilities. With probabilities, you need to understand the game and you need to cut your losses and let your profits run. There will be small gains and small losses and trades that leave you flat. These outcomes will tend to cancel themselves out over time, and you will be left with two outcomes—big winners and big losers. Money management is designed to avoid that big loser. No matter how much you analyze, try to understand, or try to control, the plain fact is that the world is too complex to consistently forecast future events. Because we will never get closer than "what is most likely to happen" as opposed to "what will happen," we need a plan with money management. There is no Holy Grail, no perfect indicator, and no certainty.

DEVELOPING YOUR INVESTMENT PLAN

Here are five basic questions to ask yourself as you devise an investment plan.

1. How much money do you have to invest or trade with? Look at your balance sheet and take just a part of what you determine is your risk capital. When I was a commodities broker, we were taught that risk capital was money that wouldn't affect your lifestyle if you lost it tomorrow. The reason you take just a part of your risk capital is that if you lose only part of your trading capital, you still have another chance to change your strategy and maybe recoup. You need to have some money left when you come back the next day.

If you have a stake, you will be able to come back. If you have tapped out, then you are out of the game. There is a second reason not to be fully invested. If you are 100% long and a new investment idea comes along that is very desirable, you will have to decide what to sell to make money available for this new idea. Having something in reserve is good in case all your open trades lose more money than you anticipated.

How much of your money or net worth to allocate for trading or investing depends on a number of factors. Consider your age and willingness to risk money; this is likely to change as you get older. Examine your motive for trading; it could be to make money, or it could be for excitement. Your occupation and the time you have available to trade also enter into the decision.

2. How much are you prepared to risk or lose? Establish an overall figure, and decide how much to risk on any one trade. You may think you have designed and tested an instant winner, but despite all the confidence you may have about making money right away, you must allow for market adversity. Typically, the loss allowed on trades is 10% or less per trade. If the stock moves 10% against your entry price, get out of the position. No matter how convinced you are of the merits of the investment or the soundness of the company, when the position goes against you by 10%, get out. Your plan might use 5% as the trigger to get out. Readers of *Investor's Business Daily* are used to reading about cutting losses at 8% below the purchase price.

We feel better when we are right, but with investing, the only thing that matters is the final result—how much money you made. Discipline must be exercised and even planned. Without discipline, you are very likely to become an investment statistic—just one more loser.

Futures traders might consider losses of only 1 or 2% of their capital on any one trade. By keeping your losses small, you can handle a string of losses without going broke.

3. What are your specific investment plans and objectives? It's interesting how people react to this question. Sometimes people respond with the comment, "I want to make as much as the market allows me." Other people respond by saying we should just let our profits run, simply trail our stops along until we are stopped out. Another way to take profits is not to get out until you see a top or bottom pattern on a candlestick chart (because they form quickly and mark reversals). While these answers seem somewhat logical and may work, one psychologist, who works with one of the most successful hedge funds, has found that goal-setting has helped good traders become even more successful. If you take the approach of deciding to just "let your profits run" and you don't have a predetermined profit objective of 25% or 50% or 100%, then risk becomes the key. I think it is better to find a target on the chart and look at risk with the target in mind. For years, commodity traders have been applying the method of taking trades on which the price objective or target is three or more times the risk. If you seek out trades with a risk/reward profile of at least three to one, and you are diligent, then you don't even have to be right half of the time to make money.

4. How do you enter your trades? What signals will you use? For this part of devising a plan, you will find a lot of books with chapters on when to buy or how to buy. What is usually given short shrift is the method of getting *out* of trades. You could use moving-average crossovers to enter trades. One moving average or two or three can be used. You could use mechanical methods like going long or short when the market makes a new 2-week high or low, or use the 4-week rule.

There is also a breakout model that was supposedly used by the famous commodity speculator Richard Dennis. That approach was to go long if today's price is the highest for 30 days, or to go short if today's price is the lowest for 30 days. This sounds like trend-following. The risk point or stop loss on a long position is if today's price is the lowest for 20 days. A short position would be closed if today's price were the highest in 20 days. Profits were taken using the same rules as for stop losses. When you think this approach through, you find that the exit rules are the same for profitable and unprofitable trades. In application, this means you are looking to catch the trending moves and to get out of breakouts that fail. The losses can be quite big, but you should still have money to commit when the really big move comes along.

Another model that is simple, elegant, and sensible comes from Stan Weinstein in his book, *Stan Weinstein's Secrets for Profiting in Bull and Bear Markets*. He used some simple tools like the 30-week moving average combined with breakouts from base formations and expanding volume to buy stocks and mutual funds as they broke out. Some methods are based on buying retracements or pullbacks to bases, but Stan recognized that some of the most powerful breakouts did not have profit-taking reactions back to the base to provide a low-risk buying opportunity.

5. How do you add to positions, take profits, or move stops? Let's assume that you bought near a breakout and the market has moved in your favor. You can increase your gains by adding to the position, but what does experience tell us?

First, always add to positions in the direction of the trend. If you are long, then add to positions on strength. If you are short, add on weakness.

Second, smaller positions or equal positions are added. If you start by buying 1,000 shares of XYZ, then add 1,000 of XYZ or less. Equal amounts will build a rectangular position, and smaller added positions will build a pyramid, with the largest position at the lowest price. Never add to your position if the market is going against you. Always let the market tell you that you are right.

ENTERING A TRADE

There are three ways to enter a trade. First, we could buy before the breakout. We might see what looks like a saucer pattern or an inverse head-and-shoulders bottom, and we pick a spot and go long. Your price risk is probably smaller at this point, but you take on a new risk that no breakout may occur or that you will have to wait for it.

A second method is to buy on the breakout. Here, your money is not tied up waiting for the breakout, but the risk increases. First, we have the risk of a false or failed breakout. This can and does happen. Second, if the breakout is good, you now have to risk more money to have your stop below the market.

A third approach is to buy on a pullback after the breakout. This method may make a lot of logical sense, but there is another problem when stocks break out and keep climbing without a pull-back. A compromise may be in order. You could buy one-third of the total position you want to establish in the base pattern, buy another third on the breakout, and buy the last third on strength. (Jesse Livermore supposedly built up his positions by fifths.)

PLACING A STOP ORDER

Before you enter a trade, set and enter a stop order. Always pick the level before you jump in, because if you try to set a stop later, your judgment will not be entirely objective. Always try to use a clear technical level for your stop, as this makes the market the decision maker. If the level is a round number or an obvious point where a lot of stops might be placed, move your stop to just above that point. This will mean you get out of the position ahead of a possibly deeper slide as a large number of stops are elected.

EXITING A TRADE

Getting out of trades can also be done in stages. One-third of the position could be sold when your profit target is reached, or on a spike day. If the market is still strong, the remaining two-thirds of the position could be held until there is a trend break, and the final one-third could be sold when a reversal pattern develops.

A FINAL EXERCISE

Look at the following charts and decide where you would go long, where you would place your sell stop, where you might add to the position, and what your price objective is.

Figure 19.1

SYSCO CORP 28.97 0.220 0.765%
D: 10/01/69 O: 0.085 H: 0.103 L: 0.081 C: 0.0955 Y: 44.85

Figure 19.2

SYSCO CORP 28.97 0.220 0.765%
D: 08/16/99 O: 15.53 H: 15.84 L: 15.19 C: 15.590 Y: 33.39

Figure 19.3

SYSCO CORP   28.97   0.220   0.765%
D: 11/14/01   O: 25.40   H: 25.48   L: 24.79   C: 25.48   Y: 32.00

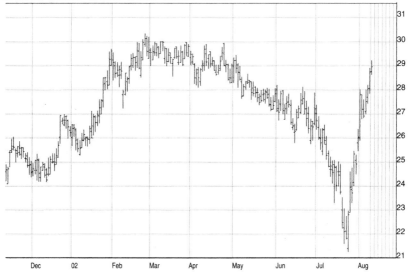

Figure 19.4

SYSCO CORP   28.97   0.220   0.765%
D: 07/29/02 9:30AM   O: 24.15   H: 24.70   L: 24.01   C: 24.62   Y: 30.18

Figure 19.1

This is a thirty-year monthly log chart of Sysco Corporation. Sysco bottomed in the fourth quarter of 1974, the last major secular stock market low. This stock has been amazing. It hardly dipped in 1987 and in the 2001–2002 bear market for most equities, Sysco basically went sideways between $22 and $30. This is what relative strength is all about. Go to a Web site and see how the company has outperformed the general market.

You could have gone long this stock anytime it traded to a new high, even though the corrections were relatively shallow, you do not have to buy a dip.

Figure 19.2

The weekly chart of Sysco Corporation has been stalling at $30 for more than a year while the stock market has made deeper and deeper corrections. This could be a triple top formation. Does the volume pattern fit? Go to a Web site and check it out. This could be a broadening pattern. A breakout over $30 is bullish and gives a target of $38. Do you remember how to measure this kind of pattern and how to project the objective? We have a target, but what do we have to risk to know if we are right or wrong?

Figure 19.3

What does the daily chart show? A V bottom. A bull pennant in August with the market testing resistance in the $29 to $30 area. It looks promising. Do we need more confidence in knowing what to risk?

Figure 19.4

Here we have drilled down to an hourly chart. On the way up we see resistance was encountered at $28, so a sell stop could be placed below what will be support (former resistance), below $28 or $27.50. You could buy this stock at $29 and add on a move over $30. A move over $30 could allow you to raise your sell stop to $28.50.

This is how you want to break down your thinking on a stock and to work through a trade. Look at a long-term chart and then a weekly, then daily, and then maybe hourly when you get ready to go long or short.

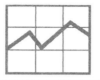

Directory

www.activetrader.com

www.barchart.com

www.bigcharts.com

www.bloomberg.com

www.candlecharts.com

www.clearstation.com

www.dorseywright.com

www.e-analytics.com

www.futuresmag.com

www.futuressource.com

www.investomedia.com

www.metastock.com

www.mta.org

www.na-marketletter.com

www.pfr.com

www.pring.com

www.pristine.com

www.prophetfinance.com

www.stockcharts.com

www.wallstreetcity.com

www.wealth-lab.com

Index